parenting delights

parenting delights

Whole Parents Complete Children

Rosalind Stone

wisdom tree

ISBN 81-8328-091-9

First published as *Just Kidding* in South Africa by Kima Global Publishers.

Published by
Wisdom Tree
4779/23 Ansari Road
Darya Ganj, New Delhi-110002
Ph.: 23247966/67/68

Published by Shobit Arya for Wisdom Tree; *edited by* Manju Gupta; *typeset at* Marks & Strokes, New Delhi-110002 and *printed at* Print Perfect, New Delhi-110064

Contents

This book is dedicated to my daughters, Nicci and Jodi —
the most precious gifts of love.
They are the air that I breathe.
God is the beating of my heart,
without which there would be no breath.

Acknowledgement

To my constant companion and guide,
beloved Master Sananda.
You were with me before the beginning of time,
I will follow you until the end
of all eternity!

Introduction

Raising Kids is Like Baking a Cake

To educate — from the Latin word *educo* means 'to educe', to draw out, develop from within. And so childhood is a time of development, of gradually expressing one's full potential. It is a preparation, not a final performance. Indeed life itself is a process of preparation, experience and evolvement.

Children need only two things — to be loved and given opportunities to acquire life skills, which are learned through living, not competition. Competition causes children to be hypercritical of themselves, which in turn stifles free expression. True education occurs when the child's uniqueness is drawn out — the ingredients entering inside to a large extent determine what comes out.

No matter how precisely you measure the ingredients, you'll probably never be able to make grandmother's chocolate cake quite the way she did. There are too many variables — the freshness of ingredients, the exact temperature of the oven, the heaviness of your hand, and, perhaps, most importantly, your expectations! The sensation of biting into a slice of grandma's chocolate cake is created not only by the act of biting, but by the companionship of loved ones, familiar smells and sounds, the sense of belonging. And there are dozens, even hundreds, of other chocolate cakes that are just as nice, but not the same!

You are the producer of your life experiences — you set the stage. If you live your life with preconceived ideas, chances are you will be disappointed. And so it is with raising kids. You have it all worked out in your head, perhaps long before the child is even conceived. You imagine that you will produce a strapping young lad who will captain the rugby team, and a pretty little girl who will steal everyone's heart and take away the trophy at a ballet school. But what you get is a son who takes after the wife's family — small and slightly built, with a passion for the arts, and a robust daughter who can hit a cricket ball clear off the field at the age of six! In real life, what you want and what you need are not necessarily the same things! So you are disappointed — you set yourself up for that disappointment by having expectations! And this disappointment can often cloud your vision, preventing you from seeing the glory within the child that you have been blessed with. Perhaps now is the right time to remind you that your children do not belong to you — they are placed in your care, so that you may guide and love and nurture them, and see them reach their full potential. Note, I say, *their* full potential — it is their dreams we must assist them in to bring into reality, not the dreams that you have for them. Your children are not extensions of yourself, through which you can realise all the goals that faded away, or re-invent missed opportunities. They are little souls starting out on their own journey. They come with a purpose and with the wisdom of the ages encoded into the very fibre of their being. And they have been entrusted into your care. How awesome is that? Don't diminish the joy of parenthood by having specific expectations, or by making comparisons; just relish each and every opportunity to share and witness the unfolding of your child's own uniqueness. Enjoy the act of parenting by allowing your child to enjoy the process of childhood.

Today's parents are overwhelmed with the results of studies that show that children need mental and physical stimulation to further normal development. This is partly the result of a generation of children raised on TV and instant meals, and who grow into unstable adults. However, in many cases, parents have over-reacted and can be accused of denying their children their childhood. Even before birth, pregnant mothers play recommended music to their unborn child. Toddlers are exposed to flash cards and structured educational toys. Children of all ages are shunted from one activity to the next. Family life becomes so frenetic that it is difficult to discern whether the competition is greatest between the children or the parents.

In a recent survey in the United States, children were asked to name the three things they most wanted from their parents. An overwhelming majority listed *time* above all else — time to chat, to play basketball with Dad, to help Mom in the kitchen, to eat as a family, and time to just 'chill'!

In children of all ages, play is the predominant activity of choice. Not only does it allow creativity, but real learning also takes place in a relaxed environment. When the brain is in a relaxed state, all experience is assimilated at a deeper level — whether this is extending the limits of physical co-ordination or perfecting higher intellectual understanding. In adulthood, all work and no play leads to a dysfunctional life, yet we believe that by denying our children the right to play, we will create a better adult!

Sometimes parents have such high expectations of their children that they lose sight of the fact that they are unique, and sometimes fragile individuals; not knights on a chess-board.

And remember that since they are not yours, they may be taken away at any time. Possibly the biggest source of regret amongst parents in late life is that they didn't take full advantage of spending time with their children, who have now either grown up or have passed on.

On watching your children grow, you will see yourself mirrored in them. You will learn to know yourself better and they will help you to grow to your full potential. Life is never a destination: as long as we are still breathing, we are still on the journey. And each and every moment of every single day is an opportunity for us to learn something new about ourselves, and to change. For it is in changing ourselves that ultimately we can change the world. The human psyche is continually evolving, allowing us not only to develop new skills and advance in technology, but also to identify more closely with who we truly are, who we want to be, and who we do not want to be, both as individuals and as the human race.

It is in giving that we receive. It is in giving to others the very things that we want and need that we attract the same things to ourselves. And in receiving, we experience the emotions, pleasurable or otherwise, which carry us to the next step in our personal growth. The emotions drive us forward, ever seeking to grasp, make real, the illusory element that would allow us to feel complete. And yet there is no completion, for in completion would be perfection, and in perfection no way forward. And there can be no end to something that is eternal, and we are eternal — our spirits have no beginning and no end, because the divine in me is the divine in you, and together we become whole. So grow with your children, sometimes drawing together like a mighty wave, and at other times becoming separated and lying quietly in little rock-pools — living together, yet existing independently, creating your own separate ecosystems which are not yours to keep, but yours to enjoy and celebrate in. Each moment of being, existing, loving, is a precious encounter with each other.

Love — unconditional love — is the most important ingredient in any relationship. It is in accepting all aspects of the other person without judgement, and at all times acting in the best interests of the long-term happiness of all concerned. To live without judgement means to be fully content with yourself, because judgement comes from comparison, and comparison from the belief that things are either good or bad, better or worse. To live without judgement means to recognise the special uniqueness of every other person you ever meet, to acknowledge their role in society, to respect them, to honour and to allow them the freedom of choice. And to do this, you must have respect for yourself.

I once surprised a client by bowing down to her in honour for being chosen to parent a mentally retarded child — it wasn't a choice the mentally invalid had made consciously, but she had surely been chosen in the divine plan because of her compassion and patience. I honoured the child who had come on such a difficult journey, and explained that without children with special needs we, the human race — would never have learned to be compassionate and gentle. To a large extent we owe the evolution of the human race from barbarians to our present state of civilisation to children such as her. The very word 'invalid' speaks volumes about our attitude towards such people in the past, for, depending on where the accent is placed, it can become 'in-valid', as of no value or importance. Surely we now know that no person is invalid or of no importance! There is no shame in being different, but there is great honour in being unique, as each and every one of us is. And there is weakness in intolerance!

To realise your full potential is the only true success in this life, no matter what your full potential might be exactly.

Christopher Morley (1890-1957) has said: "*There is only one success — to be able to spend your life in your own way.*"

I knew a family once who had allowed preconceived prejudices to bring tension and unhappiness into an otherwise perfect family, when their only son chose to become a dancer. For months the mother secretly corresponded with her son but his name was never mentioned at family gatherings. His father disowned him and his sisters were embarrassed by the implications of his passion for movement and music. Finally, the son was selected for the lead role in a grand ballet, and the mother, determined not to miss the opening night, fabricated an excuse to travel to the city. At the last minute her plans went awry and the father insisted on travelling with her. Of course, the real reason for her trip soon became apparent. Not wanting his wife to go out alone at night to a strange city, he reluctantly agreed to accompany her to the ballet. At the final curtain, the young man received a standing ovation — only his father remained seated — paralysed by pride and filled with remorse for his own stupid actions and the precious time which had been lost forever. This young man went on to dance in productions the world over, and his father became his greatest fan! You see, the father realised that scoring a try on the rugby field, or winning the chess Olympiad, or transporting an audience into rapturous fantasy, are all equal victories, moments of glory, when our true potential shines through.

Yet we judge our children harshly and make them feel inferior when they make a mistake, or choose to do something differently. If a visiting friend should accidentally carry mud into the house on the soles of her shoes, you would no doubt brush it off, saying, "It's just a little mud! Don't worry about it." But if your own precious child should make the same mistake, you would react with anger: "Look what you have done? Why are you so thoughtless and stupid?"

Why indeed! Because children are not perfect, and neither is anyone of us!

A child without guidance will grow up confused and insecure, and therefore you have not acted with her long-term happiness in mind. On the other hand, a child who is so severely disciplined that it stifles her development and blossoming of unique and precious qualities, the child will become equally confused and insecure. And so you will need to set parameters that not only allow for each individual's development, but do so without infringing on the happiness and enjoyment of others within the family.

Now, I don't consider myself an expert, though I have two wonderful daughters of my own. I have perhaps seen more of life than the average person — through the eyes of the many people who have come to me over the years for counselling and healing. And it is through my work as a holistic therapist and spiritual healer that I have gained insight into what kids — from birth to the age of 104 — really need.

Whether you are reading this as an adolescent, a new parent, or a grandparent, or a person with no family at all, you'll surely recognise yourself and your life in these pages, and perhaps, somehow, these will lead you to a healthier, happier way of being.

People, young and old, need to feel safe in the material world, secure and important in society, and good about themselves. They need to feel worthy of receiving love, and to believe that the love they have to give to others is valuable. People need freedom to express themselves, both verbally and creatively. And they need to have spirit, be inspired, and believe in a higher power.

Your true nature is fearless and filled with joy. There is an inner knowing, an unexplained power, which allows you to follow your dreams and create the reality you desire. Your personality, however, is that aspect of you which is revealed to the world and has been created by the opinions of those around you. When a child is placed in your care, you have the power to create a positive and successful being, or a broken and negative shadow. Use this power wisely, for the success and joy of your child is indeed your own.

Chapter One

All is One

Feeling Safe in the Material World

Love, compassion, and tolerance are necessities, not luxuries. Without them, humanity cannot survive.

— His Holiness the Dalai Lama

Imagine the confusion a little soul must experience at the time of birth! As a pregnant mother we have access to literature and guidance from our elders; we have the support and comfort of loved ones, doctors and nurses to reassure us. And we have a developed cognitive brain that helps us to understand what is happening, and to put it all into perspective. But the baby? A little soul finds itself developing into a human form, warm and safe within the mother's womb. It is unaware of hunger or thirst, or any discomfort but vaguely aware of muffled sounds, and acutely aware of emotional love coming to it in waves. Anyone who has ever experienced the liberation of a flotation tank will relate to the feeling of being totally without stimuli, and that is the world of the unborn child. And then the whole world goes crazy — the cushioning water suddenly drains away, the uterus which previously held it lovingly now pushes and shoves, waves of fear and anxiety reach it as the child is squeezed down a narrow passage into a world that is expansive and non-supportive. It is now that the baby becomes aware of the temperature and bright lights, strange noises and smells, and the sensation of air in her tiny lungs!

What the baby needs most at this time of adjustment is to feel safe in the material world with her family. Until about the age of seven, the issues of survival within a family structure are most important to the development of a child. These important issues are to have her primary needs met — food, warmth, security — so as to be free to explore the world around her. When these basic requirements are not met during infancy, the child grows up believing that the outside world is threatening, and fears that it may not be able to provide life's necessities for itself. All psychological and physical resources are channelled into survival, leaving no space for emotional and intellectual development. A child who feels that it doesn't belong, and is totally alone and unsupported, will later on in life have difficulty in materialising his or her own goals.

Babies are not naughty — they do not have the reasoning skills to allow them to be so. They respond to stimuli. Your baby and growing child needs to know that you will be there when he needs you — when he is hungry, wet, cold or just a little lonely. The small baby does not see himself as being separate, but feels the family to be an extension of himself. When these aspects of himself fail to respond, the world becomes a scary and unpredictable place. I have never understood the reason behind allowing babies to cry for prolonged periods.

Whatever it is that requires attending to will certainly not disappear spontaneously; instead, the small child will learn that grown-ups, and in particular her parents, are unreliable and not to be trusted!

Punctuality in all things is important, and more so for children. Children hate to be late — whether for school, a party or a piano lesson. They pick up on nuances and feel separated. Make the effort to be punctual for the sake of your children. If you yourself are inclined to be late, here's the bad news: *you are arrogant*! People who habitually expect others to wait for them do so out of arrogance, which is a symptom of other emotional issues, like wanting to control the outside world because self-control is a bit too tough!

The best place for a crib to be is right next to Mom, and if the baby still frets at night, move the child into bed with you. This way you can comfort the child without really waking up, and if you're breast-feeding, you might not even have to get out of bed at night! How can a small child or infant be expected to feel safe and secure when it is abandoned in a dark room, away from comforting voices and a warm embrace? No mammal, and few birds, would consider doing such a thing. There are even some reptiles which nurture their young through the early days, and yet we, the human race, intellectually superior, detach ourselves from our young! In all my years I have never encountered a teenager who still sleeps habitually in Mom's bed (although there's no reason why she shouldn't be there if she is ill or has suffered some trauma). Most children who are given the freedom of crawling into the parent's bed will feel secure enough to stay in their own room. Throughout life it is easier to confront the challenges before us when we know there is a safety net to catch us if we fall! You are your child's safety net; make sure there are no gaping holes.

A good routine of feeding, bathing and playing will also make the child feel more secure. Unable to ask when her needs will be fulfilled, a routine allows the child to follow the pattern and know that things are under control. In this way we teach our children that the world is a friendly and loving place to be in. It is the first lesson in organisational skills, and prepares the child for a more structured routine that life will take on when it is time to begin formal schooling. They learn to trust and respect their family members, and this lays the foundation for a happy, interactive family life.

Parents are often afraid that by giving in to the infant's requirements, the child will become spoilt and demanding. In my experience the opposite is true. The child who knows, really knows, that Mom and Dad are there for her when and if she needs them, is far more likely to explore independence. She is not afraid that Mom or Dad might go away and leave her behind or not come when she calls. Instead, she will be content to spend time playing alone, and discovering herself. It will give her a sense of being in control of her environment, and this will later allow her to set goals and realise her dreams.

I once read about a journalist who found a small child of less than a year old abandoned and crying on the sidewalk outside an apartment block. No one else seemed concerned about the plight of this infant, and when the journalist made enquiries, he was directed to an apartment on the third floor. There he found both the parents, drinking beer and watching TV. They confirmed that the child was indeed theirs, but when asked why she had been left alone outside, they became quite indignant. They claimed that she was crying because she didn't like the sunshine, and the parents maintained that it was good for her to be outdoors so that she would get used to it! For this little girl, sunshine and the great outdoors represented rejection and enormous insecurity!

There is a tendency amongst young parents to make children fit in with their own lives, rather than adjusting to suit the child's needs. Well, I hate to be the one to break it to you, but being a parent is your life now! That's not to say that you should put all your dreams on hold and have no social life, but it does mean that the needs of the family as a whole take precedence. As a new parent you should find enjoyment in your new role — change is a very positive entity, unless we resist it and attempt to remain in the past. Your children have the potential of being the greatest source of joy you will ever know in this world, so don't rob yourself of the opportunity to experience it!

Communicate with your children! No relationship can survive without proper communication, least of all the relationship you have with your children. Don't insult your children by presuming that they cannot understand you. Children understand words long before they are able to vocalise them. From the day you bring a new puppy into the home, you begin teaching it commands and rules, and conditioning it to respond to its name. After a week or two, the puppy should have a good idea of where it is supposed to relieve itself, when it is expected to quieten down, when left in a darkened kitchen, and the meaning of simple words. If you've gently pushed the puppy into a sitting position every time you place a bowl of food in front of it, it will begin to do this automatically. Yet we continue to use baby talk and treat our own offspring as if she is completely brain-dead until ready to begin school! Speak to your child — explain what is going on around her, why certain things should be done, and others avoided. Include all the members of the family in family issues.

Events such as death and divorce or retrenchment become scary only when shrouded in mystery; when the child feels confident that she is being told the truth, she is less inclined to allow her vivid imagination to run wild, creating scenarios far worse than the actual reality of the situation. When parents handle situations calmly and sensibly, children feel reassured, and accept change as an inevitable part of life, not something to be feared and dreaded. They learn to face challenges and adversity with courage and determination, rather than succumbing to defeat. And they learn the value of working as a team. It is easy to identify individuals who have had the experience of being part of a team, either within the family or on the sports field — more importantly, such individuals are able to place a value upon themselves and their contribution to society.

Where the family dynamics have broken down, youngsters may be drawn into gangs to gain a sense of belonging and importance.

You cannot give a child too much love. Even when you're angry or tired, remind yourself that you love this little person, and let the underlying emotion be one of love. The tone of your voice, the expression on your face, should tell the child, 'You are loved always and all-ways!' Make it a rule that every time you have eye contact with your child, what she sees in your eyes, and feels, is love. Allow that love to flow through into your touch — be gentle yet strong. One of the most difficult exercises in team-building workshops amongst juvenile offenders involves falling backwards into the arms of teammates, trusting that they will not catch them. Many of these youngsters have never felt the security of a firm and loving embrace. They have never trusted another on the physical level, and they're unsure as to whether they themselves can be trusted in this way.

Touch is an essential part of being in a physical body. Animals do it, naturally, giving and sharing — it is a form of communication for them. It should be for family members too. A hug cannot be put into words! Physical contact is vital to the normal development of a child. Research has shown over and over that children denied physical contact develop slowly at all levels — physical, mental and emotional. Care-givers are now employed at many of the larger children's hospitals purely to provide this contact, whilst mothers of premature babies, rather than be denied access, are encouraged to touch their tiny infants as often as possible. The 'kangaroo philosophy' recommends having the small infant strapped to the mother's body, and this has shown remarkable improvement in development and reduced mortality rates in low birth-weight babies. Many of the ancient and indigenous cultures used a similar method to carry their children, and this played a vital role in teaching the child to see herself as a part of the team. Occupational therapists working with emotionally deprived children will often teach them a form of 'self-comfort' — such as thumb sucking or stroking their own hands to assist the child in coping with insecurities.

Touch goes much deeper than simply the physical sensation. There is a sharing of energy through the human energy field that surrounds us, and the intermingling of these fields brings about a harmony which has profound healing properties. The positive effects of the presence of animals in homes for the elderly, as well as in children's homes, have been well documented. Children with special needs, including autistic children and those suffering from post-traumatic stress syndrome, respond extremely well when allowed physical contact with animals. How much stronger this healing property would be when coming from a caring parent! During my second pregnancy, I frequently strapped my older toddler to my back, which served not only to balance my centre of gravity, but also to remind her that she was no less important. When her new sister was born, it was 'our' baby and there was never a moment's jealousy.

As adults we want and need to be touched, and women often complain that their husbands neglect this aspect of the relationship. Yet, as parents we hold back, afraid that close physical contact will produce a 'softie'. Actually, I think most times the parents are simply afraid of revealing their own needs and vulnerabilities, and so perpetuate the cycle. Sometimes the reluctance to have physical contact stems from the parent's own insecurities and confusion about sexuality.

There are numerous good reasons to breast-feed a baby, and the physical bonding should not be overlooked. Too many mothers, unable or unwilling to breast-feed, deny their baby this important closeness by simply propping the baby up with its bottle, rather than cradling the child in her arms. I was fortunate to be able to breast-feed each of my children for 18 months. Towards the end of this period, the value of the nutritional nourishment was debatable. But the value of that precious time together is immeasurable.

Don't make idle or unrealistic threats, as you will be compromising your own integrity and the child will learn not to rely on you. She will learn also that it is possible to get away with not taking responsibility for her actions — later on in life, this can lead to some painful lessons. We need to make choices in life based on whether the consequences will be positive or not, not on whether we are going to be caught and punished. By explaining to a child why we don't want her to do a certain thing, we teach the child to think ahead, assess the outcome, and make a conscious choice on how to behave. Small children are usually fascinated by a candle flame, and in spite of being told, "Don't touch! It will burn you!", they do invariably test this theory for themselves, feel the burn, and learn respect for both the fire and the parent's wisdom. Of course, some parents will use this as an excuse to exert authority by punishing the child for not having listened, and not *loving the child in spite of her mistake.*

Making threats but never pursuing them teaches the child to avoid punishment by becoming devious, rather than developing integrity. There are certainly times when a smack is needed to establish authority, but never lash out in anger. Resort to physical means only when negotiations have failed. It is in the child's best interests that the lesson be learned, and that it be learned now! At times your children will challenge your authority, and you will need to defend it. Again this process is part of Nature and also part of the animal kingdom — anyone who has witnessed a lioness or she-bear playing with her cubs will have seen both the incredible gentleness and the occasional snarl and cuff.

However, if you are going to defend your position of authority, ensure that you deserve it, and have earned respect through your actions! Resolving issues through violence has never been a success, not ever throughout written history. Using violence to control your children teaches them to use violence to control situations throughout their life, and that power can be attained through external means. In truth, authentic power comes from within. Small children often resort to external power to get their own way amongst the peer groups — smacking or even biting — and the parents are nearly always totally dismayed at such behaviour. Yet, when you examine the family dynamics, you often find that physical force is used in a home, either in the form of frequent smacks, rough handling or even yanking a child's ear! Children learn by example!

Never threaten to abandon the child — we do it mostly by

transferring anger towards our spouse or circumstances on to the defenceless child! If you need 'time out', away from your spouse and/or children, announce this need and do something about it, before the pressure valve gives way and you do and say things that you will no doubt regret. On the other hand, whilst you may be tempted to abandon your two-year old who is throwing a tantrum in the shopping mall on Saturday morning, you would in fact be running away from the symptom, rather than having the courage to address the cause!

Tantrums in small children are most often a release of frustration caused at being misunderstood, or a feeling that they are not being listened to, or simply as a result of not being able to verbalise their feelings and desires. Slow down and listen to your child!

Abandoning our problems and obstacles in life is a sign of weakness, emotional immaturity, and not something that we should want to instil in a developing character. Especially in one with whom we may have to interact for years to come!

If you realise that you have misjudged a situation or reacted too harshly, admit that you are wrong! Remember that children learn by example and if you are too proud to admit to having made a mistake, your child will learn that making mistakes is something to be ashamed of, and will attempt to cover up her own poor choices. Rather, accept the responsibility, explain why you have had a change of heart, apologise if necessary, and move on! If you're not sure on how to react, call time-out, giving all parties a chance to go away and think things over, and then negotiate peacefully once everyone has calmed down. When communication is open and honest, a child will admit comfortably to having made a poor choice, and will seek your advice in putting right the matter. The more honest you are with your child, the more honest she will be with you. And the more you encourage honest communication, the less likely you are to have to punish the child — once a child recognises her mistake, admits to it and shows the intention to put it right, then there is no value in punishment. We are not seeking to 'place the blame', but rather to instil integrity. This comes from developing a sense of remorse, which is very different to guilt. Few parents derive pleasure out of punishing their children; so spare yourself the anguish rather than going through parenthood, putting out fires that could be avoided.

Your home should be both a sanctuary and a castle for all those living there — a place of peace, harmony and safety. Parents who expound "as long as you're living under my roof ..." while waving a pointed finger, make children feel as though they are there through an act of mercy, not love and belonging. It is their home too, remember, so allow them to entertain their friends, sing in the bath, beat drums in the backyard and splash in the pool! A note about pointing a finger — ever wondered why even an untrained dog responds to this seemingly inane gesture? It is because this is the equivalent of shooting an arrow into the very sensitive energy field that surrounds us all! Don't do it, except when you're feeling physically threatened and in need of some self-defence

As far as possible, ensure that your child feels safe and cared for, and that she belongs! In my experience, the long-term consequences of being deprived of this basic need to feel safe within the material world include lowered immunity, resulting in frequent infections, as well as personality disorders such as obsessive-compulsive disorders, depression, phobias and paranoia. There may also be a tendency to blame others for one's actions, rather than accepting responsibility for one's own choices in life. People deprived of this primary need are governed by fear, and miss out on much of what life has to offer.

When children are directed by fear, they will often seek the sanctuary in what they do know, rather than expand their horizons. This obviously can lead to poor social interaction and a tendency to retreat within the boundaries of the home, believing that if life is so uncertain there, how much more scary it might be on the outside! Of course, when the situation at home becomes too threatening, these children may resort to living on the streets — an indication of the appalling conditions from which they have fled.

When parents are confident and outgoing, taking advantage of all that life has to offer, children are inclined to follow a similar path.

Bryan

When Bryan first came to see me I was amazed that a body which had been so badly abused could still look relatively good. In spite of dark rings under his eyes and greasy hair which had been rather amateurishly peroxidised, his tall frame was well proportioned, his features striking, and I could not help thinking how joyful his life would have been had he made different choices. Wearing a creased, long-sleeved T-shirt and jeans to hide his skinny body and the track marks of regular heroin use on his arms and ankles, he was a mere shadow of what he might have been. Yet, shining through the sadness and disappointment, was hope! And a desire to make right his wrongs, and see his own magnificence.

A well-adjusted boy from an upper middle-class family, achieving both in the classroom and on the sports field, at age 11, Bryan had accidentally stumbled across his adoption papers while looking for something in his mother's desk drawer. Obviously feeling insecure and betrayed, he mustered the courage to question his parents, but instead of receiving comfort and reassurance, he was punished for 'snooping'. His repeated attempts to speak about his adoption and uncover the whole truth resulted in him being accused of bringing discord into the family, and upsetting his younger brother and sister.

Confused, and by now feeling totally rejected, Bryan's behaviour at home and school deteriorated, and six months later he was sent off to a boarding school. In his mind this was the ultimate rejection, and by the age of 12, Bryan was smoking dagga on a regular basis. In spite of this, he maintained good grades and his habit went unnoticed. He gradually regained his confidence, and participated enthusiastically in hostel life. Then, during the summer holidays at the end of Grade 10, he was introduced to cocaine. Bryan's father meanwhile became a very successful doctor, leading a high life with his wife. The two younger children were attending private schools and little mention was made of the 'errant son' who had been sent away. Bryan felt like a stranger in his own home and that summer, he spent a great deal of time with a relative. It was this relative who offered Bryan his first line of cocaine, and since money was no object, and his parents were only too happy to have him out of the way, the high cost of cocaine was no deterrent. Smoking joints satisfied his craving for oblivion during the week, and at weekends he treated himself to a few grams of cocaine. The dealer also introduced him to mandrax, and later, crack cocaine. Half way through Grade 11, Bryan was expelled for smoking dagga on the school premises. While he may not have been a model student, Bryan had felt secure at the school, and the acknowledgment he received for his grades was sorely needed. Many of the boys came from broken or dysfunctional homes and they became like brothers to one another. Now, once again, he was being rejected.

Not wanting their son's shameful use of dagga to become public knowledge, his parents swept the matter under the carpet, so to speak, and enrolled him at a local school. There was no counselling or therapy; in fact Bryan could not remember either of his parents even asking why, or how, they might help. His brother and sister viewed him as an outsider, a potentially bad influence, and were not encouraged to spend time with him. His new friends were regarded with suspicion and not welcomed in their home. For all intents and purposes he was expected to complete his schooling and then go away again. In spite of his serious drug addiction, Bryan managed to matriculate and register at the university. Sadly he dropped out before mid-year. Having been given the freedom of his own car and a sizeable allowance, Bryan entered the dark world of heroin.

A year later a cousin visiting from abroad persuaded Bryan to seek help, and so he spent three months at a drug-rehabilitation centre. Now he wanted to move forward. He was looking for work which would allow him to be outdoors and use his creative skills, taking him away from home. His constant fidgeting and nervous tremors revealed an extremely fragile and traumatised emotional state, and his nose was constantly running as a result of the severe long-term use of cocaine. He slept for a long time after the healing, and was truly amazed at how peaceful and whole he felt. I detected a boyish excitement, but his fear of being judged prevented him from fully expressing his sense of being loved. I always hug my clients when they leave, and most respond warmly. But Bryan, though he smiled broadly when I asked his permission, was clearly uncomfortable, feeling unworthy of such unconditional love and acceptance.

On his second visit, Bryan was far more relaxed and confident. He was washed and neat, and carried himself with a pride I'd not seen before. The week of eating fresh fruit and vegetables, prepared by the family housekeeper, had brought a glow to his complexion. A glimmer of hope now radiated out strongly, and I celebrated this transformation with him. Still wanting to move away from his family and the influence of friends, he was actively seeking employment, and possibly for the first time in years, believed that things may work out right for him. He had been thinking a lot about who he was, and using affirmations to remind himself that he was loved. He had written pages and pages in a journal, helping to shift the blame from himself to his parents, to realise that they had failed him, and that it was okay to feel rejected and angry towards them, to begin the process of forgiveness and, ultimately, healing. He also felt that it was okay to love himself, to feel worthy of happiness, and to expect love from others too. We spoke about his sexuality — many drug addicts become bisexual in their search for fulfilment, and also often give sexual favours in return for drugs. He had voluntarily been for an HIV/AIDS test and was anxiously awaiting the results. Not yet 16-years old, Bryan was having to process more emotional material than most people have in a lifetime.

This time he readily succumbed to the peace induced by spiritual healing, and when he returned from that magical place, he hugged me warmly, and with confidence and sincerity.

We scheduled a follow-up for the next week, but he didn't keep the appointment. When I called his home, they were not able to tell me where he was. Three days later he arrived on the doorstep. Dishevelled and unwashed, his hands were shaking, his eyes dull, and his spirit looked more broken than ever before. He told me a story that made my heart break, and I had a hard time retaining my composure. In my line of work you learn to hide your shock and disgust, but what he told me filled me with both despair and anger. In fact, as I write this, I am blinking away the tears.

The day before he was due to see me for the third time, he had suffered an attack of paranoia, not uncommon in people who have used drugs, especially LSD. Feeling desperately vulnerable and unsure of himself, he had begged his mother not to leave him alone at home. But she had arranged to meet some friends for morning coffee, and argued that she couldn't think of an excuse to cancel. Bryan's 'drug problem' was still regarded as a shameful secret, and she was not about to lose face within her social circle. This was, after all, his problem, not hers. The solution she came up with was to give him US$ 600 (Rs 30,000) and drop him off at the dealer's house on the way to her engagement! There could never have been a greater rejection, and Bryan went on a four-day binge of drugs, sex and alcohol.

He surrendered to the healing like a lamb going to the slaughter. But when he left, I think we both knew that we would never meet again, not in this world anyway.

I don't know what became of him, but my guess is that he chose to continue along the road of slow self-destruction that had begun a decade before and which had begun because he felt unworthy, unloved and rejected; because he perceived himself as being simply not good enough.

I think about him often, and I pray for the souls of his parents.

Chapter Two

Honour One Another

Feeling Secure and of Value within Society

We must all understand that if we are to be Divine, we must, like the Divine, love with Divine intensity and serve every sentient being on the earth.

— Andrew Harvey

There comes a time when the child begins to see herself as being 'separate'. Whilst the small baby views everything as an extension of itself, the developing child begins to realise that Mom and Dad, as well as siblings, are separate individuals, that they have their own feelings and needs, and rights within the family dynamics, or the playgroup. So whilst the child is loved unconditionally, she also needs to learn to respect the needs of others, such as appreciating that Mom and Dad deserve a good night's sleep, and being quiet in the library or church. If your child feels safe and secure within the family environment, and has learned to trust you, she will not be threatened by discipline, provided the discipline is done with love and understanding.

A child needs to understand *why* she should be quiet in the library in order for her to respect that rule of society. Our aim is to raise children who are free thinkers, leaders rather than followers, or at least, followers who have learnt to make an informed choice. "Because I said so!" has no place in reality, and especially not when raising children. It conveys two things about you — that you don't know the answer, and that you are an authoritarian but cannot justify your position! A child needs to learn to share, to see itself as part of a larger network which is necessary for life. This means not only respecting the position of others within that society, but also respecting her own place within society. If you demand privacy at times, then your children deserve some privacy too. If you demand that your children listen to you, then they deserve the same respect. How often I have witnessed small children desperately trying to attract a parent's attention, and being totally ignored! Certainly, children should be taught not to interrupt when others are speaking unless it is of extreme importance — but that level of discernment develops with time. Their reason for interrupting may not seem important to you, but it surely is to the child — perhaps she has a question about a disabled person passing by, and realises that the subject may soon disappear from view, and the chance to learn will be lost, seemingly forever! Your powers of discernment are, or should be, better developed, and you should be able to tell the difference between a pestering child and one with a thirst for understanding. Listen to your children constantly, learning the different tones of voice which often reveal more than the words themselves.

Children learn to 'take charge' of their lives by *being* in charge. Encourage your children to take charge of their lives by allowing them to place their own order in a restaurant, instead of waiting for a 'bigger' person to do it for them. Accompany your child into the sweet shop, but allow her to approach the counter alone, keeping a watchful eye to ensure that she is not overlooked or overcharged! And let her do it her way — don't hurry her, or tell her to speak up; that will come with confidence. Meanwhile it's a lesson in patience for the waitress. By undermining her ability to do such things, you are severely stunting the growth and development of her self-confidence. By constantly criticising how your children do things, you will lead them to believe that they have to repeatedly qualify for your love! Carrying this belief into adulthood will leave them vulnerable to being taken advantage of, and incapable of saying 'no'. Hard as it may be to acknowledge, you were once a child who couldn't tie a shoelace!

Allow your children to explore life's opportunities, and experience interacting with others in extra-curricular activities. Just because you think your daughter has two left feet is no reason why she shouldn't be allowed to attend ballet lessons, and what better way for her to improve her co-ordination than through the medium of dance and music? Both my daughters did ballet even though the calculations showed that they were destined to be far too tall to ever become ballerinas — but they danced in concerts and eistedfodds (rock competitions), even bringing home a few trophies. It taught them discipline, gave them the courage to go out on an empty stage (my younger daughter was just three-years old when she rendered her first duet!), gave them the thrill of being applauded, and gave me some very, very precious memories!

When they decided after a couple of years that they'd had enough, we donated the leotards and bought swimming costumes. And yes, I invested many hours and plenty of money as they followed their dreams of Olympic glory. We travelled far and wide to attend galas, and I timed more races than I can remember, rejoicing when they bettered their personal best and encouraging when they didn't. But the day came when they decided not to swim at club level any more — were they failures? No! Their swimming careers had been enormously successful, with trophies and certificates to prove it. But more important was what they had learned about themselves, other people and life! And, of course, the quality time we had spent together cannot be valued.

They went on to try their skills at cross country, biathlon, life saving, water polo, katabo — and the road of discovery continues. How often we dash our children's dreams before they've been given a chance by making comments, such as "But you can't even hit a ball!" or "You know you'll never win that race!", etc. Could you hit a ball before you learnt how? Do you think any Olympic gold medallist would have won a race without being allowed to try? And remember that these are not life sentences, they're just life! So when your child is tired of junior judo, don't force her to continue doing so until she is 21! Recognise the skills that have been learned, and move on. The fact that a child gets tired of a particular activity does not make him a failure; it makes her a mover! And the world is built on the efforts of movers! To avoid opening yourself up to anger, don't rush out and buy all the most expensive equipment for the first lesson. It is also important that children learn about commitment, both to their own goals, and to the team. By all means insist that your child honours this commitment until after the last match or the concert, but then let it go. And take the practice sessions seriously, but not so that you drag a sick child to soccer practice, or make your daughter miss her best friend's birthday celebration to attend a piano lesson. Life is a journey, don't forget; not a race!

So many times over the years I have asked my clients this question: "When you were a child, imagining the time when you would be a grown-up, did you see the journey you would have to make in order to get there, or did you simply visualise yourself as being there instantly?" Of course, we all visualise arriving there as if by magic, but in reality we know that the path may be long and winding — walk this path, stopping to smell the flowers along the way, because in reality there is no 'there'. There is only the joy you allow yourself to feel in the present moment!

It is important to remember that each of your children is special and unique. Avoid comparing your children to one another! Very difficult, I am sure, if one child tops the class and wins all the races, while the other doesn't appear to have any remarkable achievements at all! Don't point this out — do you honestly think the child hasn't noticed? We all have special talents, some take a little longer to become apparent than others, requiring a greater level of emotional maturity or skills. Looking back through history you will find that a great many highly successful and famous people only began to blossom during their adult years. Reassure the 'unsuccessful' child of your unconditional love, and your belief that she will discover her unique talents when the time is right. Ensure that your time is equally divided and encourage other children to celebrate with their siblings' successes, but guard against favouritism. Ensure celebrating achievements by all family members, however small and insignificant they may appear in relation. And be sure that the children are aware of your philosophy to prevent hurtful teasing and boasting.

A client of mine ran away from home at the age of 16, believing that she was a disappointment to her family, as she simply was not able to compete with her younger sister. In her quest to find a place for herself in society, she embarked on a journey of drugs, promiscuity and attempted suicide. Today she is a successful young woman with her own beauty saloon, having achieved far more than the younger sister, who shone so brightly as a child. Unfortunately it was probably the parents' unrealistically high expectations which caused her to seek a less pressurised existence, and not reach her own potential.

Remember, you are there to guide and direct, not instruct. Make suggestions and recommendations, rather than laws and prohibitions, and allow your child to develop at her own pace into who she wants to be!

It is during this phase of growth that the child develops a sense of self-worth, learns to set and follow realistic goals, and begins to view herself as being a valuable part of society. Emotions that arise from failure to develop in this area include feelings of inadequacy, fear of poverty or lack of wealth and dishonesty. A person who has a high self-esteem or self-worth will not find it necessary to use dishonest means to boost her own ego. This includes fibbing, gossiping, and even stealing, to make herself appear more important. Later on in life, low self-esteem often leads to self-destructive behaviour, such as alcohol and substance abuse, promiscuity, eating disorders (both anorexia and over-indulgence) and the need to manipulate and control others. Refusal to accept another's point of view, without necessarily agreeing with it, is the manifestation of low self-esteem, and the need to be right! If you recognise your own dominating nature in these words, think back to your childhood to find the source!

Feeling safe and secure within society means feeling okay about oneself in relation to others. Where there is a lack of acknowledgement and excessive criticism, the child will grow up with low self-esteem. There will be a fear of failure which will prevent the child from exploring her capabilities, and shyness preventing her from interacting and developing social skills. Never laugh at a child's mistakes or fumbled attempts — ridicule cuts deep! And if you really can't help laughing at the outcome, make sure that the child understands that you are laughing *with* her, not *at* her. Of course, if you expect your children to be able to see the funny side of their *faux pas,* you need to be able to laugh at your own mistakes too!

A child that is frequently compared to others will feel 'less than' or inferior, and begins to see her special contribution to the group as being meaningless. An inner belief of 'Oh well, if I could do it, then anybody can' will replace the joy of achievement, and such a child will not be inclined to strive towards her best. Since her efforts are not rewarded with acknowledgment and praise, the child will often resort to 'negative attention seeking' with unacceptable behaviour, since any attention is better than none at all! Alternatively the young adult may become a perfectionist, not accepting that anything she does is quite good enough and, once again, believing that one needs to qualify. In young girls this frequently manifests as anorexia or bulimia, whilst young boys may react with violent outbursts. If you are occupying a human body, you have already 'qualified', so now start living!

So much of this phase of learning stems from the self-esteem of the parents. If Mom and Dad act inferior because of their financial status, body shape, level of employment, or even cultural or religious group, it will impact severely on the child. In South Africa we witnessed the result of such beliefs, where whole generations were raised to believe that they were inferior, creating poor self-esteem and bringing with it the associated problems.

Our high crime rate is a direct result of the fact that socio-economic issues deny many children the loving interaction vital to normal, healthy, emotional development. Gangsterism, stealing and substance abuse are all symptoms of poor self-esteem and the need to control situations through violent means, or escape from a reality which holds little or no attraction. There is a need to create an external persona, since the inner persona is perceived as being inadequate. In many cases the rapist is venting his anger towards a mother who may have abandoned him, either literally or figuratively, and is an attempt to take by force what he believes he has been denied. Rape is not an act of sex; it is an act of violence, and violence stems from anger. Horrific cases of young children committing acts of violence are a symptom of a society that controls by force and denial, rather than by guiding with love, and allowing the individual to shine through.

Parents with an egotistical outlook teach their children to be judgemental, and the child might grow up fearful of not meeting their standards. Unable to secure a place within the family, such a youngster might choose to mix with 'low-lifes' in order to make himself feel better because within this group he can see himself as having status. So often these youngsters, when interviewed individually, will claim that they are 'better than' the rest of the group, and don't really see themselves as belonging there at all. It is all a matter of comparison. Alternatively the child who takes refuge in mimicking his parents will become big headed and bossy, not a good recipe for popularity amongst the other kids!

At all times remember that you, as parents, are a living example to your children. The old adage of 'do as I say, not as I do' is a totally ridiculous concept — do as you would have your children do, be what you would like your children to grow up to be, that is, themselves. My children are fully aware of the many protest marches that I have been a part of, demanding equality for all races, recognition of all religions, better pay for teachers, stricter sentences for rapists and several others. They have witnessed me physically defending a small street child from a group of older boys, and confronting a boy who was stoning a harmless snake in an act of senseless cruelty. I make a stand for the principles in which I believe, and encourage others to do the same. It has made my life more interesting and I go to sleep at night with a clear conscience. They are in no way obliged to adopt my beliefs, but they are encouraged to seek their own truth, and be true to themselves. They are encouraged to see themselves as being valuable members of the society, and to uphold principles which can, and will, make a difference.

It goes without saying that this phase of emotional growth includes an awareness of sexuality. Children begin to notice the physical differences between their parents, and their siblings. They become aware of so-called male and female roles within the family and society, and may be uncomfortable with the role that is expected of them. Children require role models. If Mom is reliable, gentle and loving while Dad is inconsistent, brutish and uncaring, it is not surprising that a young boy might prefer to emulate Mom rather than Dad. Of course, if Dad is seldom around to be a role model, it leaves the child with little choice! Dad's horror at having a son who plays with dolls and helps Mom bake, and stinging comments like, "Are you a moffie?" will hardly endear the child to his father, or encourage him to follow in Dad's footsteps. And don't use the argument that you are only joking, and that the child doesn't even know what the word means —

children are extra-sensitive to thought vibrations; they know what you're thinking, and, more importantly, what you are feeling!

Learn to tolerate who and what your children are. There are far too many prejudices in society today, too many people who are discriminated against, either individually or in groups. Think how you would feel if your own child were to lead a life of misery because of community misconceptions. Every single person is somebody's child, everyone has parents somewhere, and everyone has the right to be happy.

Children will ask questions about sex which need to be answered. Again, remember that you are setting the stage for future acts — if you are not honest and open about sex at this time, how can you expect your children to discuss sexual issues with you later in life? Don't lie about anything, including sex. Once your child has caught you out on a lie, there will always be an element of doubt as to whether she is receiving the truth. Be honest! Give your children what they need to know — the bare facts, without graphics and embellishments; just enough to satisfy their current curiosity. You will not need to teach your son how to have an erection, but you will need to guide him as to what to do with it! If they feel you have given the truth, they will feel comfortable about coming back for more as the questions arise. Don't pretend that you don't know too much about sex — you're a parent, aren't you, so how did that happen? It happened because you and your spouse are sexual beings; you have genitals and hormones and the desire to be touched and become intimate. And if your children are permitted to develop into healthy, balanced young adults, they will have these attributes too! If God had wanted it any other way, He would have made us differently, like the fish who deposit their eggs and hope that a male will swim over the spot and release his sperm into the water, and so perpetuate the species. But we are not fish, and neither are our children.

It is important that children learn that they have a right to protect their sexuality, especially with so many sexual deviants out there waiting to pounce. When one of my daughters was around 13 years of age, a man made a lewd and suggestive remark to her as she passed him in a public place. She rapidly caught up with me, and I only needed to see her face to realise that something was not right. When she told me what had happened, I went after the man and confronted him, making sure that my choice of words left no doubt amongst the curious onlookers about what had happened. Yet I created a scene! Initially my daughter was embarrassed, but when she saw that other grown-ups supported my actions, and the man was forced to leave rather hastily, she became the victor, instead of the victim. Her integrity and sexuality had been defended, and I suspect the victimiser would think twice before preying on a young girl again. She also learned not to be the victim of other people's insecurities, and that it is alright, even applaudable, to make a stand for your rights.

In counselling children who have fallen prey to paedophiles, I have often detected a sense of guilt that stems from them having enjoyed the encounters, especially where the molestation did not include penetration. They are often afraid that they themselves might be 'sexually deviant', or that they have homosexual or lesbian tendencies following same-sex abuse. And yet it is fully understandable that the child has experienced pleasurable sensations, given that the genital area is so richly supplied with nerve endings which respond to the gentle touch, and results in the release of endorphins. Both the children and their parents need to understand that the resultant pleasure was purely mechanical, and in no way exonerates the abuser, nor implicates the child.

I believe many cases of sexual abuse go unreported by the children because they are confused about their role in the matter. By being open about our sexuality we not only equip our children to say no, but also to tell us when they feel they have been violated, without having to first overcome the embarrassment of speaking about this taboo subject. I heard a horrific story of a young girl who was being molested by her step-father. Unable to speak to her mother because 'sex was not discussed', she mustered the courage to confide in a teacher, having been assured in a school talk that adults would help in such instances. But alas, the poor girl chose a teacher who was so embarrassed and horrified that she did not report the incident. Almost two years later, after repeated abuse, the mother discovered the truth. Confronting the teacher as to why she had not taken action, the reply was, "Oh, but I did! I prayed for her every Sunday in the church!" An innocent 12-year old girl had been subjected to regular abuse, and rape, because the women she trusted were unable to be open and honest about sex.

Whilst on the subject of sex, it should be mentioned that children and young adults should not be exposed to pornography of any kind. There are parents, especially fathers, who believe that this is an easy way of teaching their son 'bed manners'. It isn't; what it will do is give your son a distorted view of what women want and how they like to be treated. It is a known fact that whilst not all men who view porn are rapists, all rapists are men who view porn! And in most pornographic material there is a very important element missing — affection! At some stage your son probably will satisfy his curiosity about porn, and possibly your daughter too, but put it into perspective by explaining that sex without a level of affection is quite unsatisfying. When men argue this point with me, I simply ask how they would feel if it were their offspring performing for the cameras, or how much real respect they have for a porn star!

Many years ago a man asked if I would make a house call to see his young wife who was suffering from depression. Normally I will make visits only if the person is physically unable to come to me, but for some reason I made an exception in this case. The woman in question turned out to be a well-known celebrity, who, as a teenager, had posed for the centre spread of a 'male mag'. It had catapulted her into fame and fortune, taking her into the world of beauty pageants, acting and modelling. Although I had seen her picture, I was nonetheless struck by her beauty, and quite amazed that a woman in her position could possibly be depressed. In spite of wanting to start a family, she had recently had an abortion, unable to go through with the pregnancy for fear of losing her figure and appeal, and this was the reason she gave for her depressed state. However, as the weeks went by, it became clear that there was a deeper underlying cause, and after some intensive therapy, she admitted that she hated her father. Had I not been a psychic healer this might have come as a surprise as she always spoke most fondly of him, but now I felt we had finally got to the truth, and needed to establish 'why'. The reason was quite simple — throughout her growing years, her father had placed great emphasis on her good looks, and when, as a young and impressionable teenager, she had been asked to pose nude, it was her father who encouraged her to take the contract. She had never forgiven herself for doing it, and she had never forgiven him for not preventing her from degrading herself in this way! He had betrayed her by not protecting her from a poor choice, and by leading her to believe that her worth lay in her appearance and appeal to the opposite sex.

Within society there are great shifts taking place as to the expected roles of the male and female members of our species, but still prejudices remain which dictate that certain roles are exclusively for one gender, and even that one gender is superior to the other. Such beliefs can cause severe emotional handicaps, and a lifetime of guilt and, again, feelings of inadequacy. If, as parents, you are able to share responsibilities equally, and designate chores without being sexually biased, your children will not be intimidated by the so-called norms within the society.

Growing through this phase is based on considerable interaction with family and community members. Humans are gregarious and social by nature, and the child's ability to function within the norms of the society develops during this stage, which is of prime importance until about the age of 14. The essence of this phase of development is: How does this make others feel, and how does it make them feel about me? Am I acting with consideration for their feelings, and will my actions be damaging to, or will enhance, our mutual experience of life? 'Do unto others as you would have others do unto you' — if everyone lived by this simple motto, the world would be full of peace and happiness!

Elizabeth and Sarah

Although I have worked with different members of the same family on other occasions, this was unique in that neither of the sisters, nor their mother, was aware that the others were also clients of mine. At times I felt almost like a spy, not revealing what I knew of one of the other perspectives, and this was not always an advantage as I tried to remain impartial and unbiased. But the family dynamics were interesting and revealed the consequences of an overpowering father, submissive mother, and substantial gender discrimination.

The father had clearly been raised on the belief that men are superior to women, and that within the male world, your worth was measured by material wealth and position in the workplace. What's more, 'luck' determined the final outcome of your life, and your success or failure depended upon the measure of such luck handed down to you by a wrathful and vengeful God. Success had little or nothing to do with your own personal efforts, but rested entirely in the hands of your superiors. They were a working-class family and the father was bitter about the lot he'd been given in life. In an attempt to maintain his manly pride, he ruled the family with inflexible rigidity, suppressing both individual expression and any attempt to undermine his authority.

The older of the two daughters, Elizabeth, learned quickly that her only hope of having a better future was to marry a wealthy man. Taking full advantage of her mature figure, long blonde hair and doe-eyes, she flirted outrageously, and at the age of just 16, had an affair with a teacher at her school. If her mother was at all aware of her daughter's blossoming sexuality, she made no mention of it. Indeed, the subject of sex was never discussed at all. Her father, judging her on the way she dressed and carried herself, labelled her a 'common slut', telling her no decent man would ever want her and that she would be reduced to working shifts in a sleazy nightclub.

Before she could complete her schooling she become pregnant, married the high school dropout who had fathered the child, and began to fulfil her father's prophecy. Since her new husband had no regular income, and not satisfied that this was 'the best that she could do', she took a job at a local stationery store, and was soon having an affair with her boss. It caused the breakdown of her brief marriage, but offered no future within itself. So she returned home with her small baby, to be subjected to the ridicule and derisive comments of her father — even when she found a decent man, she wasn't able to keep him, he said. (I'm not sure of the wisdom that lies beneath judging either her incompetent husband or unscrupulous suitor as decent, but I guess it gave clarity to the father's distorted belief system.) Before long Elizabeth was once again pregnant, and although the father of the child married and financially supported her, it was a loveless union. When their son was just three-years old, he left Elizabeth for another woman. Once again her father blamed her for the breakdown of the marriage, reiterating that no decent man would ever want her.

With two small children to support, and minimal maintenance from her second husband, Elizabeth set out to prove her father wrong, and find herself a wealthy husband. Before long she was working as a prostitute, not walking the streets, but frequenting upmarket bars. It was in one such bar that she first met a professional man who was to become a regular client, and later, a full-time boyfriend with promises of marriage. He just had to break off a long-standing relationship, and since this other girlfriend was 'emotionally unstable', Elizabeth would have to remain patiently in the background until he felt the time was right. In the meantime she would visit his office at lunchtime when they would enjoy passionate sex, or wait for him to arrive at her home, late at night, supposedly unable to live without her and full of desire. He never took her out in public, and 'the other girlfriend' accompanied him to official engagements because she was 'intelligent'.

When Elizabeth first came to see me, this arrangement had been continuing for almost three years, but she felt unable to escape. If ever she demanded more commitment, he 'reminded' her about her past, saying she should be grateful that a man of his position would even have her in his bed, and threatening to tell her growing children that their mother was nothing but a common slut. And she believed him; after all, it was precisely what her father had said over and over. And he was by far the best catch she had made!

The younger daughter, Sarah, had an entirely different approach. Having seen the misery that her sister's choices had brought, Sarah set out to be the very best that she could possibly be. She worked as a part-time waitress during her senior years at school, later taking a permanent position at an expensive restaurant where she was soon promoted to junior manager. Here she worked long hours, taking pride in learning all aspects of the business. Always grateful to her employers for having given her such an opportunity, they soon began to take advantage of her, demanding even longer hours and delegating more and more responsibility to her. While her boss and his wife enjoyed the success of their restaurant, living in lavish style, Sarah seldom had time off. She soon realised from the financial records that the restaurant was doomed unless her employer stopped taking money from the till, and worked even harder to keep it going, still believing that she was forever indebted to them. But when the inevitable finally happened, she was accused of having stolen large amounts of money, and dismissed without pay. During her time at the restaurant she had moved away from home, and become engaged to be married, presenting a mask of self-confidence to the world. Now, without the security and status of her job, she was terrified that her husband-to-be would 'discover the truth' about who and what she truly was — a girl from the wrong side of the tracks, with no future or value!

The mother, Doris, was a gentle woman with a tired, submissive manner. Years of emotional abuse had left her without hope or joy. Unable to fully process the sadness of all that had gone wrong in her life, and in the lives of her two daughters, she had all but closed down all emotions within herself. Whilst the church had been a source of great strength for her, it had also been the subject of immense discord between her and her husband, with him mocking her faith, accusing it of being a crutch for weaklings, and demanding evidence of God's love within her life. But when he was forced to take early retirement because of poor health, brought on by years of smoking and alcohol abuse, he insisted that she demonstrate the 'love of Christ' and sent her to the church office, begging for employment. Here she rediscovered a part of herself that had lain dormant for all those years — she took pride in her work, and her compassionate nature soon endeared her to the parish members and clergy alike. But at home she was once more reduced to the lowly status of wife.

Over the years, her husband blamed her for not having instilled proper values in their children, and lamented the fact that he had been dealt such a rotten hand, saying that had he not married such a spineless woman he could have gone far in life. He refused to accept any responsibility for the consequences of his own actions, insisting that he was a poor victim, and claiming that had she given him a son, a child he could have been proud of, everything would have been different. He accused her of taking sanctuary in her religion, instead of facing up to the real world, and made it almost impossible for her to attend church regularly, demanding that she see to his needs, instead of serving such an unfair God. Now, weakened by his poor health, and no longer able to demand respect and authority, emotional abuse was his only weapon against his wife and the two daughters.

In all the three cases, what needed to be rectified was the negative belief which held them in bondage of being 'less than'. All four needed to carefully examine the perceptions they had of themselves, and to decide whether in fact they truly believed these things to be true. They needed to discard the thought patterns that had been handed to them, and to replace these with thoughts that recognised their own uniqueness, value to society, and their unquestionable right to be treated with dignity and respect. Part of this process was to forgive those who had played a role in keeping them in 'victimhood'. This forgiveness allows us to release negativity, thereby creating a vacuum in our consciousness which can be filled with positives/truth. The words of Jesus Christ of Nazareth, as he hung upon the cross at Calvary, sum up this process perfectly: "Forgive them, they know not what they do." For indeed, no parent deliberately sets out to disable their children through emotional abuse. Their actions stem from their own fears, and since they have not understood and processed these inner fears, they react to them, rather than responding from a place of wisdom.

In forgiveness we change the dynamic from blame to compassion. We acknowledge the deep suffering, and its terrible crippling effect, that caused our victimiser to behave in a particular way. And we begin to feel love rather than hatred and resentment. I am not sure who first coined the following phrase, but they are wise and true words indeed: 'Holding on to resentment is like drinking poison and hoping that the other person will become ill!'

I am pleased to report that Doris, Elizabeth and Sarah are all living lives filled with joy, hope and success. Doris is almost immune to the bitterness that is directed towards her by her husband. She runs a very popular creche at the church, where she is able to pour love on to her young charges, encouraging them and offering very wise advice to parents.

Elizabeth is at present not in a relationship, having discovered that she is perfect, whole and complete just as she is. For the first time she is able to spend quality time with her children, believing that her value as a parent is enormous, and is in no way diminished by 'bad' choices in her past. She is employed by a large corporation where she tackles her duties with enthusiasm and determination, and she is currently studying part-time to improve her career prospects. In simple terms, she believes that she can make it!

Sarah is learning to allow herself 'time out' — time to simply be, to enjoy fun time with her husband, to laugh at her mistakes, and to permit friends to occasionally spoil her, instead of always having to be in the driver's seat.

The father, sadly, having been reduced to a powerless figure-head, watches the world go by, refusing to accept any responsibility for the way his life has been, and waiting for the women in his life to stumble and fall, and give him back his power. But that's not going to happen because they are all proud of the obstacles that they have overcome, and proud they should be!

Chapter Three

Honour One's Self

Feeling Good about One's Self

How we feel about ourselves, whether we respect ourselves, determines the quality of our life.

— Caroline Myss

In her last year of pre-school, before beginning formal schooling, my oldest daughter wore a T-shirt on her head for a whole week. By flipping it over the back, she could create the illusion — in her mind only — of having long, flowing hair. My suggestion that she try a pair of tights instead was met with indignation — she didn't want pigtails, she wanted loose hair! And so the T-shirt with the little bear in the front became part of her daily attire, until she discovered that 'long hair' gets in the way, and so she abandoned the idea. There were many who criticised me, believing such behaviour to be rebellious and a sure sign of problems during the teenage years, and just as many who regarded me warily from a distance! But I believe in allowing children the freedom to express themselves, and if my little girl had the confidence to wear a T-shirt on her head, and not be concerned by the strange looks and comments from other children, then it was okay with me! My own mother can relate tales of frustration at my weird dress sense as a small child, and of how she eventually gave up and allowed me to go off to my playschool wearing whatever I chose, so long as I wasn't naked. And sure, this abhorrent behaviour did continue into my teenage years (in fact, some may say it continues still!) when I insisted on making my own clothes and could be seen walking through the neighbourhood in long, flowing, hand-painted kaftans. A regular hippie, you might say, and yet to this day I have never once experimented with drugs and neither am I promiscuous. You see, I knew who I was and didn't need to impress anyone, or do anything to 'fit in'. That didn't necessarily make me the most popular kid in school — people don't like to have their own insecurities staring them in the face, and there's a certain safety in blending into the crowd. But I've always been happy with my own company, so it didn't really matter. If friends couldn't accept me as I was, then they weren't worth having as friends! And so I have encouraged my daughters to express themselves freely, in order to discover who they are and who they are not!

The ability to feel good about oneself comes from trusting one's own intuitions and instincts, being allowed to express one's individuality, and having self-respect. It comes from believing in one's self. Where this belief is suppressed, there is a fear of criticism and intimidation, and often this is reversed by criticising and intimidating others, in order to protect oneself. There may be a fear of assuming responsibility, either for self, finances, actions or attitudes.

Fear of failure results in avoiding decision-making, and the inability to break free from controlling situations. All of this translates into disappointment with oneself, and the resultant anger may be released through substance or physical abuse, and a pattern of taking it out on 'helpless victims'. However hard we try to protect our children from the nasties of this world, they will, at some time, be exposed to peer pressure and drugs. Ironically the *Oxford Dictionary's* definition of 'peer' is "a person equal in rank or merit" and yet when we succumb to peer pressure, it is because we don't see ourselves as being equal to the significant others! Although the vast majority will probably experiment a little, the final decision as to whether they just 'try' it, or actually begin 'doing' it, will be made according to how they feel about themselves. The best protection you can offer your child is to send her out there with a good sense of self-worth!

Refusing to allow your children to socialise with their peer group simply sends the message that you don't trust your child, which is not only very damaging for the child in question, but also places some uncertainty on your abilities as a parent. That's not to suggest that you allow your children to do anything and everything that others are doing, but that you allow them enough freedom to build up confidence before taking the next step. And when they burn their fingers, don't punish them further; be there to support them and encourage them to re-build their broken self-confidence! Try as you might, you cannot prevent your children from growing up, but you can direct, to some extent, what they grow up to be!

If you really have a problem in allowing your children total freedom of expression, find a compromise. If you are an exceptionally tidy person with very precise ideas of how things should be, and find it difficult to leave the state of their bedrooms up to your children, offer an alternative. Small children can be given carte blanche when arranging and decorating a wendy house; older children might have a say in how the family room should look, or be given the project of livening up the walls of the garage. You'll be doing yourself a great disservice if you refuse your children a creative outlet — standing back and watching what develops can give valuable insight into your child's state of mind.

It would be remiss of me not to make some mention of cults and 'group dressing' at this point. The best way to protect your child from being drawn into undesirable networks is to instil a strong sense of self-worth, and for you to remain informed. Read magazine articles and watch TV shows, especially those aimed at parents and teenagers — just because you are 'past it' doesn't mean you should be blind to the realities of today's world! There are certain modes of dress which can be associated with cults and music idols, but often the teenager is imitating an image rather than following a philosophy — if your communication channels are open, you should know the difference. Sometimes really wacky dress styles are a cry for attention and recognition, not an indication of involvement with an unsavoury group or drug use.

Often youngsters move beyond their own comfort zone in order to force their parents to acknowledge them as individuals, and once they have received this acknowledgment, they will settle back into more normal behaviour. If you resist this shift in your relationship, your child will be forced to persist and go to even greater extremes. Use both your head and your heart when making an assessment — I have answered questionaires about 'tell-tale signs' that have confirmed I am a drug addict, serial rapist and mass murderer, and I assure you I am none of these things! Nevertheless, the type of music your children listen to and the way they dress and carry themselves can reveal a lot about what's going on in their lives and in their heads. I have reserved the right to turn off music which makes me 'feel bad' whether or not I can explain why and how, and have discouraged the use of certain emblems. Where there has been strong objection to these actions I have agreed to listen to the lyrics in full, or research the origins and meaning of an emblem, read up on a particular band's beliefs, and then make an informed final decision. Usually my initial gut feel was right and there is no argument. All the same, do remember that it is the mode of dress, or the behaviour, that you don't like, and not your child! Showing that you love them in spite of their actions will frequently be sufficient for them to drop the offending phase and move on to the next one — they're just trying to establish the boundaries, theirs and yours!

Always insisting that your children are neat and tidy, and perfectly colour co-ordinated, will not only limit their freedom in play activities (by making them afraid of getting dirty) but will probably result in your child coming home from college with dreadlocks and multiple body piercings! It's a little like cooking — keep the lid on tightly and the contents will boil over, messing the stove and wasting a good soup, whilst constantly allowing a little steam to escape avoids this over-reaction.

Regardless of how ridiculous you might think the latest fads are, hundreds, if not thousands, of teenagers disagree, so let it be! Looking back through old photo albums of your own youth usually puts this into a proper perspective!

* * *

Having found their niche within the family, and established a position in their peer group, sports team or ballet class, the young adolescent must now begin to look deeper, and focus more on self-discovery. As if puberty is not tough enough, the question now arises, 'Who am I?'

The most effective way of finding out who we are, is to ascertain who we are not. And the only way to do that is through trial and error! The fact is that truly balanced people continue this search throughout their lives, for there are simply too many options to exhaust, even in an entire lifetime, as new opportunities present themselves while we pass through the stages of life in this dimension. It's what we call growth! And certainly the most interesting adults are those who are still trying new things, venturing into different fields, and enjoying the journey! When people ask, "What are my daughters going to do with the rest of their lives?", I reply, "How should they know? I haven't even decided what to do when *I* grow up!"

Although the phases of emotional development continue to cycle throughout our lives, the main focus changes at different stages. One could say that the first phase — becoming secure in the material world — takes place from birth to around age six or seven. Then the second phase will take priority — feeling comfortable within a social setting. Since many children begin playschool at about age two, this second phase often begins a little earlier, overlapping the first, but still not being the major focus. Perhaps because Mother Nature has a wicked sense of humour — the third phase of discovering self, usually kicks in at around 14 years of age, just when the physical body is thrown into turmoil by the emerging hormones! A double whammy — so it is not surprising that many parents find the teenage years the most trying! I loved them, although they were not without challenges, but watching two special individuals emerging from the little girls I cherished so dearly, was like seeing a butterfly escape from its cocoon. Wings all crumpled, and total confusion within, until that magical moment of wonder as it takes off for the very first time!

Your teenager is likely to swing from wearing only the latest designer labels, to the brink of hippiedom (or beyond!) and back again, all in two weeks! To some extent it will depend on the company she keeps, as, having found a place in society, the last thing a teenager wants to do is to become alienated, even if it means 'swapping' friends to accommodate her chameleon act. Don't condemn it! It is not a weakness to imitate others, to try things 'their way' in order to see if it fits! If your children have been given the correct encouragement up till now, they'll be trend-setters as often as they are fashion followers. I'd far rather have a confused chameleon than a frightened sheep! The reason that we have to suffer people wearing the latest fashions, in spite of them being most inappropriate for both their figure and age, is because their parents didn't allow them to discover their own unique style! So next time you see an overweight, middle-aged woman sporting a Farah Fawcett hairstyle, leopard printed micro-mini and lime green boots, just because it's trendy, feel sorry for her — she has had a deprived childhood!

The search for self-discovery should be what drives us forward, what makes us set new goals, and what promotes change. Being able to embrace change as the positive thing that it is (after all, the only thing that is constant in this life is change, whether we want it or not!) allows us to look to the future with excited anticipation, rather than fear. And yet many people are so afraid of what they might discover if they took a peek within themselves, that they simply freeze their growth at this point, only for it to resurface with urgency at around middle age, resulting in the so-called mid-life crisis! Better to be an adolescent during your teenage years: you'll get away with a lot more!

Part of discovering who we are involves setting our own parameters. Up to now we have pretty much accepted the family norms, bending the rules occasionally to reach the norms of those in our social circle. But now it is time to set our own. These parameters are based on morals, how much respect we have for our bodies, our level of compassion for others, our sense of responsibility for our actions, and the impact they might have on those around us, as well as upon ourselves; in short, our individual sense of 'right and wrong'. These concepts have been internalised over the childhood years, failing which the adolescent (or adult!) may resort to seriously delinquent behaviour, having to experiment with extremes since there are no pre-established boundaries with which he or she can identify. The fledgling is ready to spread its wings, and attempts to fly solo. Once it is out there, there is little that you can do but watch helplessly, and pray and trust that you were a 'good parent'.

Parents, who are totally wrapped in fear about what their teenage children might be up to, are displaying symptoms of knowing that they have failed to prepare this youngster adequately for the big wide world. And the bad news is — you can neither stop the clock nor turn it back.

Your angelic little girl is going to get drunk, sometime. And your son will most likely steal the car at least once. Pretending that these things will not happen in your home simply means that you have failed to acknowledge your children as developing individuals, and that they may not be prepared to face the consequences of their actions. Initiating a discussion about alcohol and its effects, and the possible dangers such as date-rape, or the consequences of driving recklessly and destroying a life, bring you closer to the world in which your teenagers live. They'll most probably still get drunk, but they might choose to do so in the relative safety of the home with some close friends, whilst you're out. The subject of alcohol is fraught with complications given that it is a socially accepted form of substance abuse, and you cannot expect your children to have respect for either liquor or their bodies if you, as parents, do not. I have watched as fathers proudly show off their young child's ability to pour a perfect rum and Coke, and are horrified years later when the child presents with a serious drinking problem!

Children will do almost anything to gain favour from their parents, and if fetching the beer from the fridge for an already inebriated parent brings favour, then surely imitating that behaviour later on will do likewise! I'd like to suggest that all people immediately stop drinking alcohol the moment they decide to become parents (or sooner!), but that is obviously not going to happen. Nevertheless, alcohol is the single largest cause of broken marriages, wife and child abuse (physical, sexual and emotional), firearm and motor accidents, and I believe children should be protected from these dangers within their own homes at least. Remember that you teach by example, and if you have surrendered to substance abuse, whether it be alcohol, prescription drugs or otherwise, you are giving your children permission to do the same.

* * *

The next shocking revelation is that they are going to explore their sexual urges even if you insist that they are home and behind lock and key by 10.00 p.m. because where there is a will, there is a way, and where there is hormonal activity, there is desire and curiosity. I personally preferred to keep the channels of communication open, and allow a level of privacy within the home, rather than have my daughters risking intimate moments on the beach or in a parked car — there are too many tragedies where such couples are ambushed, beaten, raped and even murdered. Whether you can get comfortable with such an arrangement or not will depend on your own personal issues regarding the act of making love. And I say, 'get comfortable' because it does not come naturally to most parents!

You will need to shift your perception of your child from a 'little girl' to a 'young woman' (even the law recognises this change at age 16!), you will also need to examine your personal beliefs about sex outside of marriage, and possibly re-assess whether these still ring true. The process will probably mean going over your own sexual *history,* and putting things into a broader perspective. For instance, why did you have sex the first time — was it because you believed yourself to be in love, because your were afraid of losing your partner if you held back, because you were curious, because your friends were all doing it, or because you had a little too much to drink and threw caution and inhibitions to the wind? In dragging up these things from the past, you might well find that you need to forgive yourself, or someone else, and in so doing, give yourself the freedom to explore fully your own sexuality. We teach our children, but never underestimate the value of what they can teach us!

The discovery of self extends beyond how we portray ourselves to the outside world. It includes our ability to stand up for our own rights — the right to eat what we want, do the work of our choice, follow whatever religion we choose, and hold our own political opinions. These are the areas that are most likely to cause discord during the teens and into the twenties, and you should ask yourself, 'Am I a clone of my parents? Have I adopted everything that they believed in, or have I developed my own self? If you accepted their guidance without question, are you happy being you? Are you sure that what was right for them is right for you, and if you have never explored other territories, how can you know?' In all things allow your children to make *informed choices.* As difficult as it may be for you to watch your daughter breaking away from her strict Catholic upbringing to explore Buddhism, let her do it! Remember the controlling thing, and what it is a symptom of.

When a long line of doctors produces a son who wants to be a filmmaker, the entire family might be thrown into turmoil, but what is really important? Surely the happiness of your children far outweighs your need for 'sameness'. By insisting that they do things your way, you are saying, "I am right and you are wrong" when in reality there is no universal right or wrong! The broader your own knowledge and experience, the more credible you will be to your children, and the less threatened you'll be by their need to explore.

I once had an opportunity to discuss religion with a young Muslim man who was doing some painting of my house. He was fascinated by the variety of religious insignia and icons in my home, by the music I listened to, and the apparent contradictions. I am a child of God, Jesus Christ is my saviour and mentor, but I do not belong to the Christian church. I don't belong to any church; I belong to God. Over the years I have explored many of the world's religions — Catholic and Protestant Christianity, Judaism, Islam, Hinduism and its many subsidiaries, Buddhism and many others, such as the Ba'hai faith, Taoism, etc. I have found in all of them kind and caring people dedicated to world peace, and I have found fundamentalists who refuse to allow others the freedom to choose their own religious path. Ultimately though, there is a common thread running through all, and that is, that we are all equal in the eyes of God (regardless of how, who or what we perceive God to be!) and the overwhelming message is that we should love one another! I have taken from each that which resonates with my own inner truth, and I have developed a spirituality that is both unique and sincere, unlimited by church doctrines, and ever expanding to accommodate my developing faith.

Our discussion was the first time this young man had been exposed to the truths of other faiths, as he had been raised to believe that the Islamic faith was the only right one, and all others were meaningless to God. He was amazed to find so many truths common to more than one faith, and, I think, equally surprised to find that the subject could be openly discussed, without judgement or animosity. He was more than a little amazed to discover that I knew a fair amount about his faith, respected those who had chosen it as their personal pathway to Allah/God, but found no reason to restrict myself to a single philosophy. I often wonder where that conversation led ultimately.

Until all the religions of the world learn to tolerate all others, there will never be peace on Earth — we expect the Jews and the Muslims to live in peace in the Middle East, and we expect the Catholics and Protestants to live side by side in Ireland, but within our own social circle and family we display extreme intolerance! The same applies to cultural and ethnic differences, and if we cannot overcome our prejudices with our nearest and dearest, how can we begin to do so globally? Let go — you have taught by example, but you have no right to demand that all the people adopt your principles, not even the souls who are placed in your care! Who knows, you might discover a hidden aspect of yourself as you witness your children's explorations! Would you truly stop loving your children if they chose to follow another religion, or marry into a different cultural group? If your answer is 'yes', then I suggest that you are incapable of love, for true love is unconditional. And by this I mean that you are neither capable of loving another nor yourself!

* * *

The sacred truth related to this phase of development is 'honour one's self!' In all matters listen to your heart, and not necessarily to what has been put inside your head. Encourage your children to make decisions based *on* how they *feel*— does this feel risky, or maybe just wrong; am I dishonouring myself by placing someone else's needs and desires above my own. What is preventing me from turning back — am I too proud to admit I've made a bad choice, too shy to ask for help, too insecure to stand up for myself? The ability to honour oneself goes hand in hand with being able to honour others, the foundation for which has been laid during the first two stages of development. Whether a small child is reluctant to visit a certain friend but can't explain why, or your teenager is demanding the right to follow his heart, allow your children to respond to their intuitions or instincts, to listen to that quiet whisper within. A weakness in this facet of your personality will make her vulnerable to being victimised, and a rocky road lies ahead.

Victimisation extends far beyond the bully in the playground, and once we have learned to either accept or dish out victimisation, it is a tough habit to break. The bully is actually also a victim since no one has had the courage to stand up to him, and thus assist him in his own development. You cannot win if you are constantly trying to prove to others that you are a winner! And that is what bullies are doing — trying to gain power through external means because they feel inferior internally. The person on the receiving side is, of course, also a victim but only *because she chooses to be!* We teach others how to treat us, and by allowing ourselves to be victimised, we are saying, "It's okay to treat me this way!" A child growing up with this belief will continue to be victimised throughout life — she will not speak up when short changed or given poor service, can easily be talked into making a purchase she doesn't actually need, will be overlooked when it comes to job promotions and pay increases, and leave herself open to emotional abuse within her relationships. This is not what you want for your child!

Unfortunately there is really only one effective way of dealing with bullies, and that is to beat them at their own game! One of my daughters complained of being bullied whilst at her playschool. At first I suggested she tell the offender in a loud, clear voice to stop hitting and pushing her and at the same time I spoke to the teacher in charge about the problem. She admitted that there was a problem with this particular child, but that his parents were most unco-operative. When my daughter's requests to be left alone fell on deaf ears, I set about teaching her some basic self-defence. I showed her how to make a fist, and how to put her full body weight behind a punch. I then told her that the next time he hit her, she was to punch him as hard as she could. She did! I do not advocate the use of violence in solving problems, but sometimes one has to fight fire with fire! The bully never troubled her again and would quickly back off if she came to the defence of other children. Gradually he learnt to interact, without having to react with fear each time his authority was threatened. My daughter had given him the message, loud and clear — that she would not be treated in that way, and the other children now also felt empowered to stand up to him.

Years later as a student-waitress my daughter was short paid by the head waiter, but demanded that she be paid the full amount owed to her. When other waitresses heard what was going on, they came forward with complaints of having been short paid often in the past. The manager was alerted, the head waiter fired, and the student-waitresses received their full pay. But for many months they had been too afraid to demand what was rightfully theirs — they had allowed themselves to be victimised! Women who stay in physically or emotionally abusive relationships often do so because they do not feel they have the right to stand up for themselves, and every time the husband gets away with it, they are sending the message that it is okay for them to be treated in that way. In effect, these women are giving their husbands permission to continue with the abuse!

As parents we should guard against being victimised by our children, too. Once again remember that you are teaching by example and if you allow your children to 'bully' you, you are sending the message that it is okay to treat others with disrespect. You may also be establishing a harmful pattern for their future! As a parent you have the right to pursue your own interests and hobbies, and have leisure time to read or take a nap. If you permit your children to constantly demand your time and attention, for silly things, like "Mommy, tell Susan to give me back my crayons!", you are not only preventing them from learning conflict skills, but sending the message that you are on this planet purely for their benefit! There is no reason why you alone should be doing household chores while the rest of the family sits in front of the TV (and husbands, please note, this applies to you too!): if you allow this to happen, you are being a victim by choice, and also being a poor role model for future relationships! You are establishing a belief system within your children that will dictate their roles later on — if you have been a doormat to your spouse and children, your children will become doormats when they marry, because they see themselves in this new role, as portrayed by you!

So many youngsters, especially girls, tell me that they are either never going to marry, or only much later in life. Continuing this line of discussion often reveals a hesitancy to sentence themselves to the role of wife/mother/housewife that they see as an inevitable part of matrimony, simply because they have witnessed it in their own mother's existence. Alternatively they might be so afraid of falling into the same mould that they adopt an offensive attitude, becoming total control freaks so that they themselves cannot be controlled! I stayed in an unhappy marriage so that I could enjoy quality time with my children, but when they were old enough to see what was happening, I realised that I was sending out a double-sided message: on the one hand, I was encouraging them to act with self-respect and demand respect from others, but I was displaying the opposite in my relationship with my husband. It was time to get out! I had allowed myself to be the victim as a tradeoff, but I was aware of the fact that it was my choice to remain in the relationship, and so to some extent I was only a partial victim.

In other areas of my life, I demonstrated behaviour that showed that I refused to be taken advantage of. A friend once sent her son off to school, wearing a soiled and crumpled shirt. She had recently separated from the boy's father, who had been extremely chauvinistic. She was working two jobs to meet the family needs. The children were required to help with laundry, but one Monday morning, the son discovered that he did not have a clean shirt, having left one lying on his bedroom floor, and the other squashed into a tog bag from the week before. I know of many mothers who would have hastily rinsed and dried a shirt, or rushed around to borrow one, but my friend made her son accept total responsibility for his circumstances. It was humiliating, of course, but he never neglected his chores again. He began to treat his Mom with a great deal of more respect and today has grown up into a wonderful young man who will make an exceptional husband for some lucky young woman! Perhaps I should mention that this woman was a kind and loving mother, and had acted not vindictively, but out of necessity under the given circumstances.

And so the essence of this stage of development is to learn to honour oneself, which necessitates that we honour others — 'as we sow, so shall we reap'! When we have an attitude of 'I'm okay, you're okay!', life ceases being a competition and becomes an harmonious co-existence, the common goal being that each individual attains her highest potential, whatever that should be. Each of us can be likened to a single cell within the body — each cell has specific functions to perform, not only for its own good or for the good of the organ of which it forms a part, but for the entire body. Failing this, a part of the body may become unhealthy, and the health of the whole body will ultimately be affected. And so it is with each and every human being — we all play an integral role in maintaining the balance and vitality of the human race. If you let yourself down, you let down humanity. If you desire to heal the world, heal yourself! To accept and love others, accept and love yourself!

Sharon

Sharon first came to see me during her mid-twenties. By this age she should have developed a sense of belonging and purpose in the world, learnt to interact socially and have a fairly clear idea of her own identity. Instead, I was faced with a severely emotionally-retarded young woman with a very distorted view of reality. She also showed signs of long-term malnutrition. Her hair was as fine as a small child's and totally lacking in lustre. Dark rings around her eyes stood out prominently against her slightly jaundiced complexion, her lips were cracked and raw, and her nails bitten almost to the quick. There appeared to be little or no love for either her body, or her own self.

Although she had made the appointment herself, she now seemed afraid to talk. Watching her fidgeting with her hands, and noticing the almost continual sniffing, I broke the ice by asking whether she was taking drugs. Perhaps because there was no judgement in my voice, she broke down and sobbed. I believe it was the first time she had cried in over 10 years.

Sharon had been the oldest of five children in a lower to middle-class family. When she was just eight-years old, her grandmother passed away, leaving the grandfather alone in a large rambling house. In order to take care of the ageing man, and because it made economic sense to do so, Sharon and her family moved into his home. At first it was exciting to have a bedroom of her own, although the younger siblings still had to share. Also, since the grandfather was at home to keep an eye on the children, Sharon's mother was able to work full-time, and the family was soon enjoying luxuries they'd not previously been able to afford. But these luxuries came at a price, and Sharon was the one to pay.

After about 18 months, shortly after her tenth birthday, Sharon's grandfather began to sexually molest her, coming into her bedroom at night and fondling her. When she mentioned this to her mother after several weeks, her mother accused her of fibbing, and told her to stop making trouble for the family. The abuse continued for six years. During this time it progressed from him fondling her to him insisting that she touch him. Later he would masturbate in front of her, perform oral sex on her and expect to have the 'favour' returned. At the age of 13, she experienced full intercourse for the first time, and the grandfather continued to 'educate' her. He would tell her that she should 'remain his little girl' and when she began to menstruate at the age of around 14, he became angry, demanding to know what he was supposed to do now! She was made to feel dirty during her menstruation, and guilty that her body repulsed the old man. Instead of offering some respite from the abuse for a few days each month, she was subjected to cruel verbal abuse. Sharon began to fear for the safety of her two younger sisters, and set about ensuring that his needs were satisfied in order to protect them. But when she reached the age of legal consent, after six long years of regular abuse, she believed she had the right to say, 'no'! Determined to protect her sisters from this monster, she confronted her parents with the truth, although she had on many occasions suspected that her mother was aware of what was going on. Having repeatedly rehearsed the scene in her mind, she was nevertheless totally unprepared for her response. She was told that her sexual favours were in lieu of rent, and that if she refused, she would be responsible for the family becoming homeless!

Sharon ran away from home that night, hitchhiking across the country to begin a new life in Cape Town. She had left a note for her younger sisters, aged 14 and 11, warning them to lock the bedroom door at night, and to tell the police if their grandfather should ever do anything to them that they didn't like. We were to discover later that the old man had suffered a stroke only a few months afterwards, possibly caused by the stress of wondering whether the abuse would be reported, leaving him a virtual invalid, and sparing the other children the horror of his sick behaviour.

Meantime Sharon found herself in a strange city without money or friends, and torn between her own need to escape and the fear that by leaving she would cause hardships for the rest of the family. Since her childhood her development had been so severely interfered with that she had few social skills, and absolutely no sense of self-worth.

Because of her 'dark secret', Sharon had been a loner at school and had never made any close friends. Her academic advancement had been stifled to the point that even her basic skills of reading and writing were minimal, and because of her extreme shyness her teachers had been inclined to overlook her poor performances. The only thing she knew how to do was to sexually please a man. She also believed that she had an obligation to 'support' the people around her and which was made worse by the guilt she felt at having 'abandoned' her own sisters. It was perhaps inevitable that she should become a much sought-after prostitute — her expertise and youthful body were a great attraction, and her ability to use her hands to both relax and stimulate gained her a regular clientele within a few short months. She was soon earning enough to rent her own flat, but her sense of obligation to others meant that there was a steady flow of 'freeloaders' staying with her and living off her income.

Before long Sharon was using drugs on a daily basis to mask the horror of her reality, smoking dagga throughout the day, and often sharing a joint with a client. When some of her clients expressed an interest in harder drugs, Sharon began to deal in cocaine, ecstasy, acid and crack cocaine. Because her grandfather had been a heavy drinker, she herself never drank alcohol, and had difficulty being with clients who had been drinking, but the drugs made her feel as if her life was not really happening.

Although she was seeing up to 10 clients a day, she would offer sex to anyone who showed her kindness, both male and female. She was drawn into the world of hard porn films, and, ironically, this was to be her saving grace. It was on the set of one such film that she met a young cameraman from her hometown, and learned that both brothers and one of her sisters had also been drawn into the world of drugs, and that the older of the two boys had already had a few scrapes with the law. Overwhelmed with guilt at having deserted them, and believing that she was responsible for their present situation, she resolved to get herself cleaned up, and go to their rescue.

It took three sessions for her to tell me the whole story, with her arriving on a high for the second session. I agreed to continue working with her on the condition that she be totally honest about both her drug use and her sexual favours — not so that I could judge or punish her, but so that she would have to face her own disappointment with herself, and learn to make 'better' choices. I offered suggestions on how to dress less provocatively, encouraged her to take a 'regular' job as a waitress, taught her how to nurture and care for some plants in window-boxes at her flat, and opened her up to the joys of keeping a daily diary in which she could express her emotions.

She was surprised to discover that as a resident of the city she was entitled to a library card, and she soon became an avid reader, to some extent using this as a form of escape. She had to learn that it was okay to say 'no', and to trust in her ability to earn enough on a daily basis to take care of her needs. I told her over and over that she was loved, and had her repeat the affirmations and scriptures confirming that God loved her, had forgiven her, and needed her to do some very special work for Him. I had no idea what that 'special work' might be, but she needed to believe that she had a purposeful future towards which she should strive. She was like a child, putty in my hands, but I had to mould her very carefully, allowing the wounds to heal and not negating the reality of what her life had been. And I wasn't there all the time to guide and reassure. There were many occasions when she stumbled and fell, becoming impatient with the progress and losing faith in herself.

Almost five years later, the road to self-discovery continues. Scars of this magnitude take time to heal. Sharon no longer works as a prostitute, and although still fairly promiscuous, is more discerning than before. Her use of drugs is limited to dagga smoked 'recreationally' as she still will not take alcohol. Although she has made, and maintains, contact with her siblings via e-mail, she has yet to make the long journey home. Since the day she ran away almost 15 years ago, she has had no contact with either of her parents.

Chapter Four

Love is Divine Power

Feeling Worthy of Love

We have all been created for the sole purpose to love and be loved.

— Mother Teresa

Much of the development up till this point has been about the outer world — our interactions with others, establishing a place for ourselves within the community, and developing a sense of self or ego. But learning about love takes us into our inner world — a world based entirely on emotions and perceptions over which we alone have control. Learning to give and receive love comes as a culmination of what we have discussed up to now, and includes love of self and life. It arises from learning to give and share, being concerned for others, and the recognition that although we may not be the centre of the universe, we do nevertheless play an important role in the bigger scheme of things. It comes from understanding the power of love and the development of an inherent sense of right and wrong. Some children are naturally sensitive from a very young age, with an active conscience, but many others live purely by taught behaviour until they reach young adulthood. In most countries the courts of law are more lenient with offences committed by those who are considered under-age, or minors, because it is assumed that their own conscience has not yet been activated.

Lack of love leads to self-centred, thoughtless and demanding behaviour, whereas abuse of love leads to an association of pain with love, causing a cycle of receiving and giving abuse in its many forms. Parents found guilty of physically abusing their children almost always claim they did it out of love, and in a strange distorted way they did. It was an attempt to make the child perfect by erasing every tiny little 'fault', thereby making the child 'lovable'. It is a cry from their own sad hearts to be perfect and lovable themselves. It arises from a belief that you need to qualify for love, and that is simply not true; if you are here, you deserve love! When I meet a person whom I find difficult to love, I remind myself, 'If he's good enough for God, he's good enough for me!' And that's the truth, however horrified you may be; God loves all of us equally! He loves you no more or less than the rapist or murderer. If your greatest sin has been to use a four-letter word under your breath, the power that forgives you is the same power that forgives a drug-dealing gangster for his wrongs.

Love grows from forgiveness, and the knowledge that in each and every moment we have the choice to forgive, and move forward in love, or remain locked into that moment, and thereby carry it with us as emotional baggage for the rest of our lives.

As children, our reactions to circumstances and situations are fairly spontaneous, and the entire range of emotions is expressed — confidence, hope, fear, anger, despair. As we develop emotional maturity, we gain the ability to maintain a more even balance, being able to quickly assess the consequences of a particular response, and then react from a basis of choice rather than reflex.

Ultimately, where a person has not learned the value of love, the quality of life will be diminished. As emotions see-saw from highs to lows, positives to negatives, they interfere with the ability to remain focused on our intents and desires, and, therefore, our ability to steadily improve our quality of life. There may be a desperate search for love, and then a rejection of it due to a feeling of unworthiness or finding it unsatisfactory. This, of course, begins a cycle of 'looking for love in all the wrong places' because ultimately love exists within ourselves. Hostility and meanness will take the place of sharing, with resentment when others receive love or recognition. An inability to rejoice at the success of others stems from a deep-seated belief that 'there is insufficient to go around', whereas in truth the universe is one of abundance and we need only to believe in ourselves and see our self as being worthy in order to receive. There will be an inability to forgive, harbouring of anger and sorrow, and growing lonely and bitter. There will be an inability to enjoy life, brought on by a belief that we need to 'earn' and repeatedly qualify for love. Until we are able to respond from the heart, our behaviour will be intellectualised, usually resulting in a reaction based on fear rather than love.

Of all the emotions, the energy of love needs to be kept in perfect balance. Giving too much to others, and not being able *to* gladly receive, will reduce the joy of living. Giving without receiving often places us in 'victimhood' which is in itself very damaging, and is a sign that we simply don't feel worthy of receiving. How do you feel when paid a compliment? Are you able to accept it graciously, or do you feel embarrassed and quickly change the subject? Are you able to say 'no' when your schedule is already full, or ask for help when you're just not able to manage? You are worthy of love, and of receiving, and the most effective way of instilling this belief in our children is to demonstrate it — by giving it to them through word and action.

Leading through example encourages our children to express their love for others through words and actions too. This way they will be able to offer compliments and praise to their friends and classmates without hesitation. They will take pride in their achievements, and enjoy the moments of success without becoming vain and egotistical.

Taking without giving will eventually cause the stream to dry up, and without love there cannot be happiness. So often we are faced with stories of elderly folk who have been abandoned by their families that we find it difficult to comprehend such behaviour. Certainly I have encountered many old people who do not appear to 'deserve' such cruel treatment, but I have also met some who have created the situation purely through their own selfish behaviour. Making demands on others without ever giving of yourself leads down a one-way road, and finally to a dead end. Quite literally, the more you give, the more you get, unless you yourself are refusing to accept the love coming your way due to a deep unconscious belief of unworthiness. This may sound unlikely, as you will assume that we all do want love. And yet wanting love and being able to accept it are two quite different dynamics. The ability to receive the love offered to us is often impaired by our own suspicious nature, assuming that love must be bought, or mistrusting another and not being able to accept that something can come from nothing. Each tiny act of kindness is repaid, perhaps not by the person to whom you give, but somebody who will return it.

Issues of low self-esteem, past hurt and unforgiveness stand in the way of love, and in a person's ability to grow to her full potential. Where the heart is filled with disappointment and pain, there is little room for love to enter!

In working with girls who have prostituted themselves, I commonly encounter a difficulty within them to accept love. They simply do not know how to 'feel' love coming from another person, as 'love' has always been a material exchange, not an emotion. Regardless of the circumstances which lead them into this field of work, there is always an underlying subconscious belief that they are worthless, 'less than', and therefore not deserving of love.

The emotions released during sex are among the most powerful known to mankind, but ecstasy need not be limited to sexual encounters — the ecstasy of love can be experienced when looking at your newborn baby sleeping or watching the sun set on the ocean. Your experience of ecstasy is dependent only upon your ability to release your most powerful emotions!

Love is an action, not a word. Anyone can say the word, although there are those who won't — it is a single syllable with no difficult letters. We have all laughed at movie scenarios where a man or woman has not been able to say, "I love you." It has been written in dozens of scripts over the years, and most of us can relate to it as there is an understanding that this is an immensely powerful emotion which should not be taken frivolously, nor the word spoken without sincerity. People who are capable of saying, "I love you" without really meaning it are generally emotionally immature, not able to *feel* the emotion that the words invoke. But the *action* of love is more complicated, and few have the skill to fake it. When you love someone, you want them to be happy, not just in this moment, but forever. You do things which will bring them joy in the 'now', and which will ensure their happiness in the future. When you love someone you naturally want to spend time with them, just be with them and also learn more deeply about what makes them tick. When you love someone you allow them the freedom to grow and develop, and stand in awe of all that they become. You treat them with honour and respect. When you love someone you choose your words carefully, acting with compassion and empathy as you feel their pain as if it were your own. When you love someone you give unconditionally, and there is no such thing as sacrifice, because anything is a small price to pay. Indeed, the word 'sacrifice' should never be linked to the emotion of love. Sacrifice is defined as giving up something in the expectation of a reward. In love it is more accurate to use the term 'renounce' to describe that which we willingly abandon, since renunciation relates to giving up something in return for another which is of far greater value, albeit in the long term — acting from the heart, giving of your time and energy, not expecting anything in return, but simply because it brings you joy! And when you open your heart and start giving love, you also open yourself up to receiving. Loving someone comes from a feeling of self-worth while controlling someone is based on a fear of being surpassed. When you love yourself you do all of the above for yourself, and more! Only when you have learned to love yourself can you begin to love others.

When we were growing up my Mom used to sew most of our clothes and handknit our jerseys. She'd buy yards of fabric and, in no time, all four of us would be wearing look-alike dresses. They weren't necessarily fashionable, and sometimes it was annoying that we all had similar clothes, but they contained an energy of love that no off-the-peg garment could match. And when Dad fixed things around the house, he sealed them with his own special brand of love, and being a DIY (do-it-yourself) enthusiast, our home resonated with his love.

A group of very enterprising scientists measured the vibrational frequency of certain emotions, recording them on specialised equipment, and then creating an average. They were able to obtain a pattern for sadness, for joy, for grief, anger and love. And then they went a step further — they went into a large art gallery and measured the vibrational frequency of the energy radiating from some very old and famous paintings! And guess what — the paintings vibrated with the emotional state of the artist at the time the artwork was done! The artists had quite literally infused their handiworks with their own emotional energy, which had remained entrapped for many decades, and in some cases, hundreds of years. Further tests on handcrafted furniture, beaded garments, handwoven rugs, carved wood and all sorts of artefacts revealed similar emotional energies. Personal belongings collected from war museums revealed suffering and sadness, and religious icons held an energy of religious ecstasy or immense peace. We are all, to a greater or lesser extent, able to pick up on such residual energies, immediately feeling comfortable or perhaps ill at ease when entering a strange room or building. Children, and animals, not having favoured one of the senses over another, are usually very perceptive — you will seldom succeed in concealing your true feelings from a child.

The point I am trying to make is that those odd creations your children bring home from the playschool, or the hand-painted birthday card, or even the batch of flopped cookies, are treasures! The hot soup you prepare to welcome your children home after a wet weekend out camping, or the relaxing bath after a hard game of rugby, or her favourite dessert on your daughter's birthday — all these things carry with them a vibration of love, which is quite literally food for the soul! I have a habit of adding a 'pinch of love' to everything I cook or bake — it reminds me to be aware of acting from the heart. And I guess that is why throughout history even the finest restaurants have been unable to compare with 'Mama's cooking'. You yourself will surely have felt the difference between a gift which was specially chosen with care, and one bought hurriedly at the last minute. Maybe you have noticed the difference in energy of something you have purchased yourself compared with that of an identical object given to you by a dear friend! If you have ever been separated from a loved one, you will no doubt have instinctively clasped the long-awaited letter to your heart, even before opening it. You would have 'felt' the love without having read the written words. Make sure that 'you come from the heart' in all your interactions with your children.

Modern lifestyles tend to be very demanding, and it is easy to give our children the impression that the time spent on transporting them, helping them with a school project, or even watching them try on dozens of pairs of jeans, is time wasted. It is not — it is time spent being a parent, and being a parent is surely the most honourable of all roles! Believe me, you will look back on these so-called mundane tasks some day and wish you could have them all over again. One of the most difficult things I have had to come to terms with was the death of my dear friend's son at the age of two. My own daughters were toddlers themselves at the time, and the pain that I felt for my friend was quite unbearable. And yet in a strange way, I am eternally grateful for the experience, for it served to remind me always how fortunate I was to have my children with me still. Whenever I became impatient with not being able to 'do my own thing', or felt exhausted after a night spent nursing a sick child, or even exasperated at having to deal with teenage problems, I reminded myself that my friend, and many others like her, would gladly have changed places with me. Learn to live so that no matter what happens, you will have no regrets! When my own father passed away, it left a huge void in my life, but not one of regret, for I knew I had been a loving and caring daughter, and he knew well how much I loved him. Not long before he died, I received a letter from him in the mail, although they lived not far away. It was a letter thanking me for loving him, and reminding me how much he loved me. I know that he wrote it down on paper because he would not have been able to say it without becoming tearful, and in his upbringing he was taught that men don't cry. I cried when I received it, and I am crying now. It is one of my most treasured possessions! Don't be shy to express your love, and don't be shy to express your joy at receiving love either! When your young child surprises you by bringing you cold tea and burnt toast in bed, don't fret about the mess in the kitchen. The mess can be fixed a lot easier than a wounded heart!

We demonstrate our love for our children in the little things that we do for them, whether it be redecorating a bedroom or leaving a small chocolate on their pillow with an 'I love you' note. We also demonstrate it by not doing things for them! By insisting that they tidy up themselves, be responsible for feeding their own pets, or apologise when they have hurt someone's feelings, we teach them about the exchange of love, and the love that they have to give is valuable. What's love got to do with tidying up, you may ask? It's a little act of kindness to show how much they love and respect you, so take note! And if their idea of tidy does not quite match with your own, focus on what they have done, rather than on what has been left undone. There are many ways to train a dog, but by far the most effective and pleasurable is the 'reward' method. The reward may be a pat, a gentle encouraging voice, an enthusiastic vocal praise, or a biscuit, or whichever way it encourages the dog to want to please you. When you call your dog and it responds only on the third call, you don't punish it for the times it failed to respond; instead you praise it, thereby instilling a desire to want to come to you when called.

I know a very lonely old woman who constantly complains that her children never phone or visit her, yet when they do call, she goes on and on about the fact that they should do so more often! It is sc unpleasant for the family members that they avoid contact even more so! Focus on the good, and the bad will shrink away in the face of love!

Love for oneself is an essential survival tool — people become hopeless when the situation around them appears irreparable, unless they have learnt to love themselves enough to move on. In loving ourselves we recognise our right to happiness, and are able to muster the strength from within to drive ourselves forward. We acknowledge our birthright to a life of happiness, health and abundance — the Creator loves us all equally; no one person receives special treatment while another is denied. If you feel you are not getting your share, look inside for the beliefs which are blocking the flow of goodness into your life.

Health conditions relating to the heart and lungs are often a manifestation of our inability to give and receive love. In older women this may also manifest as breast cancer. In children, however, it can usually be identified as asthma, bronchial difficulties and pneumonia.

Antibiotics and antihistamines may well alleviate the physical symptoms, but a high dose of love and recognition will treat the cause!

In relationships we are often able to transmit love as a form of energy to a loved one who is down and out. Almost like the jump on starting your car from another battery, this love can help to lift someone out of depression and transmit into hope — enough to get them running on their own steam again, provided they believe they have a 'battery' within themselves. Looking at homeless vagrants I often wonder if only his circumstances caused this person to be deserted by his friends and family, or also his own belief in himself. Have you ever considered that giving small change to such a beggar is reinforcing his belief that he is no good and therefore can hold him in a bondage of dependency? Genuine love brings a broader perspective — give a man a fish and he will eat for a day; teach a man to fish and he will eat forever! When we sincerely love another, we constantly, in all our actions and words, remind that person that they are special, indeed, that they contain within them a Divine spark, and that if they would only believe in themselves, all things would become possible.

Loving oneself is not limited to expensive shopping sprees and extravagant trips to the hairdresser — this is using outside, or physical, means for self-appreciation, which relates to honouring oneself. Love is a far more powerful force than appreciation, and loving oneself enables us to literally let go of our past hurts, to love ourselves enough to forgive ourselves for having been a victim, or a coward, or for disappointing our self in some other way. This comes from emotional maturity, and until our children have developed this to some level, we should act as the booster to help them along the way. When we act from an angle of self-appreciation, we treat ourselves to a chocolate;

when we act with self-love, we pass up on the chocolate knowing that it is not conducive to reaching our goal — proper weight!

There are many support groups for a myriad of emotional conditions, most of which begin with a confession, aimed at the group, but in reality to coerce the member into making an admission to himself. This comes in the form of a statement similar to 'I am an alcoholic or 'I am a survivor of child abuse', or rape, or incest, or divorce or whatever. These programmes are successful to a point, as healing begins with acknowledgment that the problem exists, and that this aspect of your life has played a part in moulding you into the person you are. However, there must come a point when you love yourself enough to see yourself as being far more than just that one aspect.

Having examined your pain, taken note of your options, and gained strength from those who truly understand where you have come from, you need to get on with the act of living, and not stay stuck in the process of remembering! At this point you shift from being victim to victor — having taken the lessons and used them to grow beyond your initial weakness, you stop being the 'trauma' and start being 'whole'. When your child picks himself up after a fall and continues to finish the race, he is loving himself. He sees himself as more than 'the fall', does not regard himself as 'damaged goods', but rather as the hero who was not intimidated by adversity. To give your children a sense of this value, you need to live it yourself!

Our time on Earth is limited. Within the realms of personality, we give ourselves moments of pleasure — moments during which we abandon our cares and worries, let go of our inhibitions and just allow ourselves to 'be'. In the spirit realms we find that our soul has given us a brief time in this world, within which we experience the sensations brought to us through the five senses. And within which we have the opportunity to experience the emotions of love, for ourselves, for others and for life itself.

Not one of us knows when our time will be up. Ensure that you live each moment as if it were your last, and in your dying know that you loved, left imprints in the hearts of others. Die with a song of love in your heart, for love will carry you gently into the everlasting.

Michelle

Michelle was raised in an extremely wealthy family, and as the only child, was heir to a sizeable fortune. She was attractive, young, intelligent, had a home of her own and drove a luxury car. Because she received an ample allowance from her parents each month, it was not necessary for her to work and her life was quite devoid of purpose. She was unable to sustain any relationship because although she could buy the affection of almost any man, few men could afford to buy her affection in return. In Michelle's mind the exchange of love was measured in monetary terms.

From a very young age Michelle had been used as a puppet in her parents' stage drama. Always immaculately dressed, complete with pigtails and ribbons, frilly socks and patent leather shoes, she might just as well have been kept in a show-case, having to endure hours of sitting silently at long dinner tables, listening to the incomprehensible chatter of her parents and their high society friends. Her bedroom was always neat and tidy, and the toys were more a part of the decor than playthings. Her routine was rigid, and paid nannies 'loved' her by preparing her bath, bringing her meals, brushing her hair and tidying up after her. She never enjoyed the freedom of baking a batch of cookies, or even making a peanut butter sandwich. Even during school holidays, she was expected to be properly dressed for breakfast, whether or not her parents were there. Her childhood paintings and drawings were filed neatly away, rather than being pinned up or stuck to the fridge door. She would never have dreamed of actually giving her mother or father a gift made out of pegs and cardboard, or a hand-drawn card. The value of a gift depended on the price tag and which store it had come from. Her own gifts were beautifully wrapped in some store, and often picked out by the staff rather than her parents. Nice girls did not run through the house or make noise; she took piano lessons, but was not allowed to attend ballet as her parents didn't feel she had 'the natural talent'. She attended expensive private schools and was driven by a chauffeur; her parents felt it quite unnecessary to become involved in her school activities and would send a donation rather than attend a school fund-raiser. On the few occasions that she had the chauffeur to transport the team or classmates on a school outing, she felt embarrassed as no eating was allowed in the car, and the girls had to wipe their feet before getting in. She could not remember an occasion when her parents made any effort to socialise with her friends' parents, although most were also from wealthy families. Even when their social activities did include other families with children, Michelle was discouraged from doing anything that might spoil her clothes. A typical symptom of such smothering is childhood asthma and chest infections, and Michelle was no exception, frequently developing bronchitis. For this reason she was not allowed to play outdoors in cool weather, and was constantly warned not to get out of breath. Her life was organised so as to cause as little inconvenience to her parents as possible. In short, there was no genuine love, no sacrifice, or even commitment, either in time or emotions.

So Michelle found herself approaching her thirtieth birthday, lonely and unfulfilled. She had no desire to have children as she could not see the point with no evidence of her own existence having enhanced her parents' lives in any way. She had recently ended a relationship of two years — the longest yet — because of financial disagreements. As a result of her upbringing, she believed that if she contributed more financially than her boyfriend, she must obviously be loving him more! His acts of kindness had no real value for her, and when he insisted that an evening out be his treat, she felt that the restaurants were cheap, and took that to be an indication of his level of love for her. If she felt the need for physical contact, she would pay for a massage or facial, and intimacy was regarded as being somewhat of a messy affair. She ensured that all household expenses were shared equally, so she maintained an account of every payment, thereby forcing her boyfriend to work extra shifts in order to meet his commitments. When they entertained, she would do so lavishly, shopping at exclusive malls and setting the table with silver candelabra and all the trimmings with which she had been raised. Friends were not encouraged to drop in, as she needed time to prepare adequately, and everything had to be equally reciprocated, with the result that many of her friends drifted away, unable to maintain the standards set by her. She bought extravagant gifts, and then became angry when she received gifts of lesser value.

When I first suggested that she become involved in voluntary work for a charity, she asked what there would be in it for her. I said, "You'll feel good inside! You will feel that you have a purpose in life, a reason to get out of bed in the morning!" She couldn't understand this argument.

I persisted, "When you die, who are you going to leave all your money to? What value does it have if it has never brought you or anyone else any joy?"

On her next visit, she brought me an expensive gift and asked, "Doesn't this bring you joy?"

I agreed that it made *me* feel special and appreciated, but asked how it made *her* feel. She didn't understand!

I asked, "Does it make you feel warm inside, does it make you feel happy to see my happiness, or do you just think that in some way you have 'bought' me for a while longer?"

Gradually she began to grasp the meaning of what I was getting at, and our long journey to put her in touch with the world of emotions began. Feelings had never come into all this before as they held no apparent value for her. So she had stopped paying any attention to them years earlier.

She had never regarded herself as unloveable, because she could afford to buy 'love' but now she began to see herself as both unloveable and unloving. Where she had been numb before, she now found herself angry at her parents, furious at having been denied real love and the opportunity to be a child, to experience friendship and heartbreak, success and even failure. Her life of almost 30 years had been a sterile existence with so many lost opportunities. She felt betrayed by all her friends and lovers, who should have told her, or warned her. She even blamed money, agreeing that it was the root of all evil, and even threatened to turn her back on it and live in abject poverty. When she finished being angry with the world, she directed her anger inwards for having allowed herself to be a victim, for being too blind to the truth. And gradually she began the process of forgiveness, taking each moment as an opportunity to experience emotions, pleasurable or otherwise. She cried, she laughed, she drank too much and spoke loudly, went to cheap cafes with plastic tablecloths for a snack, and even ordered 'take-out' pizzas to entertain her friends! She bought a coat from a factory outlet and tipped the parking attendant, and that was the moment of enlightenment — she felt good inside! The attendant's joy was infectious, such that even the other attendants nearby celebrated with him. They cheered and danced and sang together, rejoicing at his good fortune. Passersby stopped and smiled broadly, infected with the happiness of the occasion. She had paid, not for an object, not for recognition, not for friendship, but for joy! And not for her own joy, but that of a total stranger. And inside, her own joy was exploding, unencumbered with an expectation or reward. As she opened up, she used her asthma pump less. She no longer needed to visit her doctor in order to feel cared for, nor monopolise the local pharmacist with her petty health problems. She could go to the supermarket in a tracksuit (okay, so it was a designer label!) and get her hands muddy pottering around in her garden. She watched the plants grow, and realised that they didn't grow because there was a gardener; they grew in spite of there being a gardener!

Had Michelle not learned to exchange the energy of love freely, her health problems would most likely have progressed into high blood pressure, angina, cardiac disease, and even breast cancer — the very problems that her own ageing parents were now facing.

Michelle is still single, but not because she cannot find a suitable partner. She isn't even looking for anyone right now; she is simply enjoying discovering her self. She has adopted a motley assortment of stray dogs and cats, packed away the bone china and crystal in favour of handmade pottery and painted ceramics, and serves fresh salads and herbs from her vegetable garden. She has let go of the past, and now feels pity for her parents, who have clearly been the losers, and she refuses to explain her actions to them. Michelle lives because living is fun. She even burnt her account of credits and debits during a light-hearted moment with friends. For the first time in her life, Michelle feels whole and independent with her own bank balance. And her home is filled with fun and laughter, and love!

Chapter Five

Surrender Personal Will to Divine Will

The Freedom to Be

You know that all that you do is synchronised with God's work, because you are at harmony, and every single activity of your life is involved in the fulfilment of your purpose.

— Dr Wayne W. Dyer

We have already looked at the freedom of creative expression and this is really just a portrayal of the development within and into the outer world. The 'freedom to be' extends far deeper, beyond the weird and wonderful hairstyles and outrageous clothes. The 'freedom to be' is surrendering to our inner being, and allowing our soul to take us gently down the river of life. It is based on trust — the trust that we have for ourselves, the trust that we place in close friends and family members, and the trust that we have in humanity and 'the system'. These are the issues that were discussed in the first three chapters of this book, and which constitute the development of our personality. When we are able to base trust on these levels, we are free to trust on deeper levels. And the 'freedom to be' is based on trust in a Divine plan, whether you see it as being conducted by a Supreme Being, or driven by the aspect of yourself that is eternal. It is the belief that there exists a spiritual world of which we are a part, and where we extend far beyond the boundaries and limitations of our physical body and the material world which we perceive through our five senses. It is the ability to step back and look at the bigger picture and thereby stop 'sweating the small stuff'. We no longer see ourselves as being in competition with others; we are simply in life with others! We learn how not being true to ourselves is dishonest and therefore ultimately damaging to those around us, and most certainly to our self.

How foolish it would be for the acorn to ignore the infinite intelligence within itself, which directs its growth and development, and manifests as an oak tree. If this driving force were to be ignored, and the acorn were to aspire to be a pine tree instead, there would simply be no tree at all! The acorn is wise, or perhaps just faithful and trusting enough, and it simply grows to be what it should be. Why then do we believe that we know better than the infinite intelligence that directs the functioning of each and every cell within our physical body, and indeed holds the planets and the stars suspended in the sky? Listen to the promptings of your own inner voice.

Failure to do so manifests in frequent throat infections and laryngitis. When these inner promptings are suppressed for long periods, the thyroid may become either over- or under-active; even neck and shoulder problems may arise indicating problems with our true self.

If you know in your inner being that you ought to set something right, apologise perhaps, or have an opportunity to explain and gain clarity, then resist doing so out of pride or fear. It will manifest in the throat, neck or shoulder area.

For many people, surrender to the inner will comes only much later in life, often only after the so-called mid-life crisis, but the foundations are laid during childhood. The less baggage the person has to carry into adulthood, the more free she is to begin the process of surrender. The more secure children feel, materially and emotionally, the more inclined they are to 'let go' knowing that the universe is finely balanced and that the tide will turn. Richard Bach, most renowned for *Jonathan Livingston Seagull,* tells in the first chapter of *Illusions* about the little river creatures fighting against the natural flow of the water. If you have not read both these books in the past year, I urge you to do so immediately! They are two of my favourites and I gain new insight every time I re-read them. When you are able to 'let go', to surrender to your inner being, you give your children the freedom, and permission, to do the same. In this way you open the gateway for your child to reach her own full potential. Life develops a purpose and no goal seems unattainable. Give your children the gift of 'freedom to be'!

It becomes apparent in psychological examinations, and to a lesser degree in such things as aptitude tests, whether a child has been exposed to faith. It matters not which religion, doctrine or philosophy forms the pillar for this exposure; what is important is that the child has been given something to believe in, and has experienced at some level the peace and harmony attained only during spiritual ritual and surrender. Science has spent countless hours and plenty of money trying to formalise and precisely measure the power of thought, which is, in fact, faith. For centuries wise men (and women, although they were seldom acknowledged in the patriarchal societies) taught that 'if you can perceive it, you can achieve it' and 'if you think you can, or you think you can't, you're right' and many more such phrases which have become so worn out with use that in many cases the depth of their truth is no longer recognised. The Bible (Hebrews 1:11) says, 'Faith is the substance of things hoped for, the evidence of things unseen.' Ponder on this for a while, and you will find that what scientists have been trying to prove, in their so-called breakthrough studies, is not a new theory after all, but a simple truth. Scientifically this power is attributed to thought being a form of energy, which is the cause, and since cause and effect constitute the law of Nature, thought has power.

Psychologically the 'power of positive thinking' is well documented, both in overcoming mental illness as well as physical disease. In religion the outcome of prayer (thought, essentially, since words must be preceded by thought) is attributed to the amount of faith that backs the prayer. Spiritually it is accepted that the energy which radiates from every living being is directed by the thought or intent of the individual, and is therefore as powerful as that person's 'faith'. Faith, then, is the extent to which we believe in ourselves as being a powerful aspect of 'all there is', rather than powerless victims of an unfair system called 'fate'.

The difficulty arises when our conscious thoughts are not in harmony with our subconscious beliefs, which have been moulded through our growing years. Take a moment to close your eyes and to 'feel' your reaction to the following statements:

- "I attract money and success."
- "Age is a state of mind."
- "Some people are born lucky."

Chances are that the first two made you feel uneasy, not resonating with your subconscious belief system, while the third statement 'felt' true! This is the result of conditioning — repeatedly hearing your parents say things like, "Hard work is the only way to get money", or "Not everyone is destined to succeed", or "You can't avoid the ravages of time", or even "I can't be expected to do that any more, I'm getting old, you know!" And finally, instead of acknowledging that someone has remained focused and determined and reaped the rewards, we pass it off as being 'lucky'. Be careful of what you say to your children — your own negative and limiting beliefs were probably handed down to you by your parents, and by passing them on, you are putting a lid on your children's spiritual development and their ability to become co-creators in the dance of life. You shatter their dreams for in a very subtle way your negative statements destroy the stuff that dreams are made of— positive thought!

We have been created as perfect, whole and complete, harmonious and finely balanced. Our natural state of being is one of peace and joy, but this equilibrium is disturbed by both negative inputs and negative beliefs within our conscious and subconscious minds.

When our own life is dictated by our fears (fear of love, for instance) and the belief that we are just tiny ants running chaotically around on the face of the planet, until such time as the inevitable happens and our bodies surrender, and then there is nothing — when we live this example, the process of life appears to be quite pointless. And thus the world has created a generation which believes that the one who dies with the most toys is the winner! It is also a generation plagued by depression, suicide and chronic disease. Clinical studies have reflected that people with a 'spiritual anchor' are less likely to suffer from high blood pressure — I believe that lack of spirituality is a factor in many more modern illnesses.

Failure to develop in this area will result in a fear of expressing needs and opinions and an inability to ask for help which may be seen as admitting weakness. Such people are often unable to cry, or express grief and sorrow, and will suppress their own creative urges. Chronic or repeated bouts of tonsilitis and other throat infections, including laryngitis or a raspy voice, are tell-tale signs of repressed emotions in this area. In many indigenous tribes, headaches arising from the base of the neck are an indication that the sufferer is not living according to the wishes of the gods and ancestors — that their life is not 'on purpose'. Learning to express who we are, based on our inner knowing, is imperative to health and longevity.

Every single soul occupying a body has a purpose — a very special and unique purpose which will assist in the evolution of humanity. The first step in believing this is believing in a 'bigger picture'. The acceptance of our spirituality is essential to getting our lives to be 'on purpose', to following our destiny, also known as the Law of *Dharma*.

For decades people have searched for ways of discovering their own unique purpose in life. Visits to clairvoyants, tarot-card readers and astrologers are often part of their quest to reveal the inner being and unravel the puzzle. Please don't misunderstand me — the value of guidance obtained from these means can be immense, but the real truth, the whole truth of who you are, is to be found deep within. In *Conversations With God,* Neale Donald Walsch writes: "If you don't go within, you go without!" Profoundly true words!

When you begin to live life as it is meant to be — on purpose, you will discover a passion and enthusiasm previously not evident. There are many ways to go about this but the simplest of which is to stop and think, and answer a few basic questions. You will know instantly whether your life is *on purpose* or not.

- Think back to your early childhood: what did you aspire to be? What role did you play in your favourite games? What activities did you choose during your quiet time alone?
- Imagine you have passed on, and are now, unseen, listening to people speaking at your funeral. What would you like folks to say about you at your funeral, and how would you like them to remember you?
- Don't beat yourself up over the things you have left undone up till now, but make a promise to yourself *to get your life on purpose!* This might involve a career change, taking up a new hobby, ending relationships which are not giving you the freedom to be yourself, changing personality traits, re-assessing your financial status so that it reflects who you truly are — a unique being with the ability to do, be and have everything you desire or any number of things. Having identified who you are supposed to be, take a few moments to reflect on these things each time you reach a crossroad on your path through life. Before deciding which way to turn, ask yourself the following questions: 'Does it contribute to my life's purpose?', 'Do I feel a real desire and passion to do this?' and 'Is this just about making a living, or is it about making a life'?

Having mastered this habit, you will encourage your children to live life according to their own inner plan and guidance, irrespective of all social pressures or prejudices.

In truth virtually every adult who has ever sought my assistance has presented the problem of not being on purpose! In some cases they are simply unhappy about what appears to be a pointless existence; in others, it is because they have developed a burning desire for change, which they can neither understand nor direct. Or perhaps they have come simply because for some time they had felt that something was lacking in their lives. This inner prompting to take up the challenge of who we are destined to be is continuous, but to some extent we are able to satisfy it by moving in some direction, rather than standing still. Imagine our lives not as a direct route from A to Z, but a complicated map with dozens of options available to take us to the next point, interspersed with crossroads, traffic circles and even multiple highway interchanges. When one reaches such a junction, one must go somewhere. It is simply not wise to continue going round and round the traffic circle! Take a turn, any turn, but for goodness sake keep moving forward, for this at least offers an opportunity.

Once one understands his or her purpose, it is easy to choose the appropriate path, but until then, the choices are overwhelming and confusing, at times even frightening. In simple words, this is because we have become the *role,* rather than the *actor!* As with an acting career, each and every role we play, however small, brings new skills, gradually equipping us to take on the next, and the next, and the next, role. An actor who plays only one role limits and confines himself, never expressing his own full potential.

When a woman reaches middle-age and her children become independent, she often finds herself without purpose. The role she has played for so many years is now redundant, the show has been cancelled, the audience has gone home. And, instead of looking enthusiastically forward to future roles, the actress believes that *she* is redundant. Her life becomes empty and her self-esteem is shaken because she no longer knows who she is — the truth is, she is who she has always been, but because she has played the role with such dedication and enthusiasm, she has neglected to nurture her relationship with herself. She is no longer able to see beyond the role and into her whole persona. Of course, this is in no way unique to women, nor is it confined to this single phase in life. Men frequently find themselves in the midst of a similar dilemma — nearing retirement, no longer in a physical condition of power, having to step aside for young blood moving up the ranks with fresh ideas. It is at the crossroads of life that we are forced to ask. 'If I am not who I have portrayed myself to be, who am I then?'

In the same way when children pass from one phase of growing up into the next, there is confusion — a certain reluctance to let go of the known, to move out of the comfort zone within which they have operated for a while, and leap into dark and shadowy waters. If I am not the girl with the longest hair, or the boy who can hang upside down the longest on the jungle gym, then who am I? If I am not the fastest sprinter, or best piano player, or part of the basketball team, or even if I am no longer an ordinary scholar, then who am I? If I am no longer a child, but not yet an adult, then who am I? Many youngsters struggle with this transition, especially when progressing from junior to senior school, or graduating from school altogether, and the only solution is to trust the foundation you have given your children, and allow them to go off and explore. Nevertheless, it is important that these youngsters do have a solid foundation of who they think they might be, before being given total freedom. Perhaps one of the most common reasons for young girls rushing into marriage is the need to 'become someone' — to take on a new role, without having to muster the courage needed to *create* a new role. The same applies to youngsters who, having just achieved relative freedom, are drawn into cults, not trusting their own ability to create a new life for themselves.

Exploration encompasses, by virtue of what it is, uncertainty. And because of our own self-doubt and fear-based personalities, uncertainty is commonly regarded as 'not good'. Suddenly the parameters and boundaries, which have helped to define the growing child, are removed. It is no longer sufficient to draw their identity from the success of their parents or the good name of their school. The strengths which identified them at school — top marks in mathematics, waterpolo team, drama club or whatever — are no longer applicable in the world outside. The young adults now have to portray their inner being, creating their own success and 'status'!

As difficult as this transition may be for the young child, it can be equally distressing for the parents! Since their children are no longer clearly defined, many parents are anxious to 'place' their children securely into the next slot. This is done by pushing them to study for taking on a sensible career, or take up an apprenticeship, or find a steady job, albeit mundane and unsatisfying. Anything, as long as the child can be clearly identified according to a particular category — student, junior clerk, whatever. Parents are generally happier about relinquishing control provided some other form of control comes immediately into effect! I am not suggesting that youngsters be allowed to pass their time at home indefinitely without contributing to household expenses; on the contrary, I insist that they be made to go out and explore! And as long as they do not get stalled at a T-junction, and are not going round and round the traffic circle of life, they are going somewhere! They are *acting out a role*; they have not become the role, nor are they limited to that role. They are experimenting, and learning and trying to see what fits. And when it fits, feels comfortable, feels right, they will know that their lives are on purpose!

Most parents brace themselves to face the challenge of their children entering the adult world, but are quite unprepared for the enormous emotional upheaval that children experience when progressing from junior school to high school. Having established themselves within the group at the junior school, and having attained a level of importance purely due to the fact that they are in a senior class, they are now relegated to the lower rungs of the social ladder once more. If the children's self-esteem is centred in their ego — the perception that others have of them rather than the deep knowing of the potential that lies dormant within — the child is likely to display more radical teenage behaviour. This is indeed a phase during which the child is most susceptible to outside influences and peer pressure. By instilling a strong sense of self-belief much of the teenage turmoil can be avoided. This belief should not be limited to the characteristics which are currently developed and active, but should include faith in one's ability to become more than what is currently apparent.

The 'freedom to be' is all-encompassing, and if you have thus far lacked the courage to examine your own limiting beliefs, you will not be able to lead by good example, and will be sentencing your children to a somewhat sterile existence. If you are not comfortable with your own company, with solitude, chances are you have not yet connected with your spiritual side. I am sometimes criticised for the amount of time I spend alone, by myself. But in truth, I am never alone, I am *with* myself. If, as an adult, we are still controlled by what others think, and see money as having power rather than being simply a currency (energy!), if we regard life as a destination and not a journey, we have no Spiritual Quotient. Some years ago, academics were thrown into turmoil when the Intellectual Quotient (IQ) was challenged as the ultimate measuring tool, and the Emotional Quotient was introduced into the system. More recently the Spiritual Quotient has been accepted as being an integral part of this measuring system for measuring the 'whole person'. It is this connection to our spiritual aspect that guides us towards finding our life's purpose.

This expression of our inner being takes many forms. If our lives are truly on purpose, it will be reflected in our choice of work, as well as how we spend our leisure time. We will feel free to socialise with others who reflect our inner self, and to express ourselves through art, music, dance and laughter. If, as parents, we fail to give expression to this inner self, our children will believe such activities to be of no value and consider them trivial. Few people will deny that watching children play with free abandon, lose themselves in the excitement of a visit to the beach, or spin round and round in the pure, simple joy of the moment, is precious.

How often do we release our inner child? Old movies that showed people dancing and singing in the streets, often in the face of great adversity, were hardly an accurate portrayal of life. Yet, when watching these films, most of us wish we had the freedom and confidence to express ourselves in a similar manner. When last did your children hear you sing, or see you dance with joy? When last did you allow yourself to be totally caught up in the joy of the present moment? When last did you embrace the Dance of Life, with all its possibilities? When last did you allow yourself the 'freedom to be'?

Once we are able to identify ourselves with these aspects which bring inner peace and joy, through listening to the guidance we receive in quiet moments of reflection, we are able to surrender, and our life takes on real purpose. We begin to live according to our Truth, with every thought, word and action displaying our inner being for all the world to witness. The reason angels can fly is because they take themselves so lightly!

Jolene

There is really little that is unique about Jolene's story. In fact it is almost a perfect example of not knowing one's purpose in life. An attractive woman approaching her fortieth birthday, came to see me with the hope that I might in some way be able to condone, give her permission even, to have an affair with a man she had recently met. This is not uncommon, by the way, as many people like to be able to shift the blame for their choices in life, rather than have to internalise the consequences and deal with them. Blame is *being lame about my empowerment* — not digging into the inner reserves and making things happen in one's life, but rather searching for excuses outside of oneself as to why they are not happening. And so Jolene arrived with a long list of reasons why she should be permitted to have this affair — she had married young, her children were demanding, her husband was focused on his career, her best friend had an affair which made her marriage stronger, she was bored, needed time for herself and so on. There was only an ounce of truth in the whole long tale — she was bored! Bored with the role which she had chosen and unable to see that she could expand that role, or even play more than one role at a time.

As the only daughter in the family, she had been raised as 'Daddy's little girl' — picture perfect and treated like a princess. She had performed well academically at school but felt it was beneath her to work up a sweat in any form of sport. Since sport or any physical challenge is frequently the first opportunity to test ourselves, she had missed out on a vital phase of personal development. Always very neat with her hair drawn back into a perfect ponytail, she carried herself with an air of smugness. (This emerged when she began to write a journal, retracing her steps and examining the choices which had brought her to this sterile point in her life.) She married within a year of finishing school — the time had come for her to spread her wings and find her true self, but since the role that had been given to her was so comfortable, and she secretly feared that if she looked within, she might find nothing at all, she sought instead a 'new king' so as to continue her role as a princess. Her husband doted on her, constantly telling her how lovely she looked, and buying her expensive clothes, and fine jewellery. He even bought her a luxury sports car which he couldn't afford, when she complained of not feeling 'special' enough. Within the first couple of years of their marriage, she had run up enormous debts and they were forced to scale down their expenses considerably. Still she refused to find work, and her husband became more and more focused on earning enough to keep her in the style to which she had become accustomed.

Married to a man who enjoyed the outdoors, hiking and mountain hiking, as well as regular workouts in the gym, she herself was never seen without make-up or well-maintaned hair and properly manicured nails, even though the family budget was fairly tight. She refused to do housework and showed absolutely no interest in the garden. When they started a family, she insisted on having a full-time nanny, and was herself always well groomed. In fact she was so desperately trying to hold on to the role of being a princess, that she lacked character and personality. Being Daddy's little girl was the only thing she had ever allowed herself to be and now it was, quite simply, not enough.

She was so concerned with her outward appearance that she was actually unable to have any fun! But admitting that, and summoning the courage to change it, was altogether too frightening!

I was more than a little surprised that she had kept her second appointment. Nevertheless she arrived, carrying a pile of books for my approval (the child in her!) and her diary, which was never intended for me, or anyone else, to read. I noticed that her make-up had been toned down. She had done a fair amount of crying at the first visit and had left with her face smudged and blotchy. She was so excited that I couldn't help comparing her to a child enthusiastically tackling a school assignment, or someone planning a long-awaited vacation. The concept that the answer to 'who am I' lies within, and not in someone else's biography, was a little hard for her to grasp — she was looking for someone to emulate, a new hat to wear. She admitted that over the years she had often 'copied' a person whom she had admired — either her dress code, or manner of speech, or even the decor in her home. Now she was searching for an invisible and totally unknown aspect of herself!

The next few months were extremely tough for Jolene. She knew she didn't want to go backwards, although the old comfort zone was beckoning. But she didn't know where she was going to either! Her husband felt very threatened by this emerging stranger and tried his best to push her back into the role that he knew and understood, and to a large extent, controlled! Friends and family joked about her mid-life crisis, shedding a negative light upon it rather than an encouraging and positive one. Even her teenaged children began to feel insecure about this 'new Mom', especially the daughter who had thus far also been raised as a 'princess'. This was possibly the most emotional aspect of Jolene's self-discovery — realising how she had oppressed her own daughter, trying to undo what she had fought so hard to create, and at the same time process her own guilt! She took another look at the seemingly perfect relationship between her own Mom and Dad, and came to the painful realisation that her Mom was dull and shallow, and that her father was a controlling and narrow-minded chauvinist. She looked through fresh eyes at the women her two brothers had married, and was embarrassed to find that they were almost exact opposites to what she was — vibrant and outgoing, adventurous and fun-loving. Jolene felt foolish — she was seeing herself for the first time and what she saw, made her ashamed. She wasn't a princess; she was a doll — lifeless and empty inside!

At the age of 40, Jolene now timidly began to explore different ways of being. She joined a gym class, where for the first time she could laugh at her own imperfection and she began to develop her physical co-ordination. She experimented with painting classes and pottery workshops, losing herself with the same intensity as that of a child discovering clay for play and unleashing a creative streak that she had never before acknowledged. She made new friends, entering into relationships on an even footing rather than seeing herself as being superior, and began to form a bond with her sisters-in-law. Even her own brothers now recognised her as a whole being, and were excited to discover a new dynamism in their sibling interactions. She changed the hairstyle she had worn for decades, and became comfortable wearing jeans and a sweater. She even reported that their love-making had taken on a new depth as she was no longer trying to maintain an air of being a lady!

Finally, the butterfly was emerging from the cocoon! It was enormously gratifying to watch Jolene revel in her new-found 'freedom to be!'

Chapter Six

Live in the Present Moment

A Lesson for You from Your Children

This moment is God's gift to you; what you do with it is your gift to God!

No man is an island — not one of us lives totally independent of the other. No matter how financially independent or socially withdrawn we might be, our life is affected by those around and the collective consciousness of all the different categories into which we fall. Regardless of how peaceful and comfortable our own existence may be, subconsciously we are influenced by the events around us. Whether this is political upheaval, economic depression, racial prejudice or any other uncertainty in the community, it will have a bearing on our subconscious mind. Any suggestion in the media of a possible shortage — whether it be of a particular commodity or economic depression — sparks a spending spree of note. Irrespective of the likelihood of you and the family actually being affected by this projected shortage, you may well find yourself stocking up a commodity that you would not normally purchase! In the same way you might be tempted to overbuy an item simply because large billboards proclaim that it is being sold at a 'bargain price' — in reality this bargain price may be only a few cents less than the normal selling price, but you will respond to the collective reaction.

The subconscious is much like a finely-tuned computer system, accepting all and any data that is captured by it, and in no way discerning between fact and fiction. Thus who we are, and the choices that we make moment to moment, are directed to a large extent by the information stored within the deep silent levels of our subconscious mind. When we remain consciously aware in each and every moment, we are able to filter and censor the information which is captured and stored by the subconscious mind, making deliberate assessments and deciding for ourselves whether a particular information resonates with our own personal truth or not. If, for instance, we have been raised to believe that the world is a scary place, full of struggle and strife, but through our own personal experience have discovered that this is untrue, we can block such negative inputs from impacting our perception of reality, provided we live consciously in the 'now'. Only through living purely in the present moment are we able to make conscious choices, de-automate our actions, and perform everything with intent and purpose. Mindfulness creates an opportunity within which our lives become more orderly; we manage time more efficiently and, most importantly, we no longer allow ourselves to be manipulated into giving our power away to negative emotions.

Remaining mindful allows us to take advantage of the space between stimulus and response, and in this space to consciously make a decision which will be for our highest good and that of all those concerned.

Living mindfully means adopting the belief that the past has no power over us unless we give it the permission; that the future is uncertain, but directed by the choices that we make in this moment, and therefore this moment is the most precious thing we have! We decide in this moment whether to be angry, or whether to cherish what the moment has to offer. It is in these single moments that we choose whether to make a hurtful and angry comment, or whether to remind ourselves that we love this person, and therefore to act with patience and understanding. We can equate this to the credits and debits in the relationship, where it is obviously necessary to have more credits than debits to maintain harmony.

It is not necessary to be highly informed about matters metaphysical in order to recognise the effects of negative emotions upon ourselves. We are surely aware of how anger and resentment make us feel in contrast to how joy and forgiveness impact upon us. Spending time worrying and fretting, often over things that may or may not come to pass, is extremely tiring. Wallowing in self-pity, or being governed by fear, drains us of both energy and enthusiasm. These things affect not only our moods but have a profound effect on our physical bodies too. Increased adrenalin as well as insulin levels cause damage at the cellular level, predisposing us to illness and disease. Raised insulin levels promote unhealthy weight gain, with all its consequences. When we are emotionally stressed, the metabolic rate initially rises in preparation for the 'flight or fight' response. When the stress continues for prolonged periods, the metabolism slows down, reducing the breathing rate and overall energy levels. Stress is the underlying cause of many physical and mental conditions, and can be most effectively managed through the use of mindfulness.

You can struggle to row upstream to get to the picnic spot you missed, or you can go with the flow, staying close to the shore and looking out for another, possibly better, spot. The choice is yours!

If your relationship with your children, or anyone else for that matter, is not what you wish it to be; you have plenty of opportunities to make it good, however hopeless it might seem at the time. If you consistently make deposits into a relationship account, you will eventually get into a positive balance!

There are four main factors contributing to our general well-being — these are food, water, air and attitude. Whilst the first three are obviously essential for maintaining the physiological functions of the body, attitude dictates the flow of both energy and life force through our whole being, and determines the perception that we have of life itself, and therefore our level of enjoyment and success.

A positive attitude is essential for a long and happy life filled with health and vitality. There are some things in life which we do not have the power to change, though we do have the power to decide how to respond to the circumstances. "Grant me the serenity to accept the things I cannot change, the courage to change those things that can be changed, and the wisdom to know the difference!" Change what you can, and change your attitude towards the things that you cannot change. Develop a sense of humour, lighten up a little — things go wrong, children spill milk, teenagers make some odd choices in life, then choose a positive attitude — choose to laugh at things.

The art of being mindful is quite simply taking control of your mind as opposed to being controlled by them. At any one moment there may be several dozen thoughts moving through our awareness, and since we are not able to examine each one individually, many have a negative impact upon us without us being consciously aware. By disciplining our minds and thus managing our thoughts, we are enabled to make sensible choices on whether to react or discard the particular thought.

Young children are naturally mindful, becoming totally engrossed in what they are doing in the moment, or captivated by the scene being played out before them. Sadly, as children grow, they are encouraged to disperse their attention, and indeed learn to multi-task. By the time we reach adulthood, we are able to eat without chewing or tasting, watch TV and read at the same time, follow a recipe and listen to our children, and even drive a motor car while speaking on the telephone! This may appear to be a positive thing, yet in actual fact it means that we are denying ourselves the pleasure which could be derived from any one of these activities. A large contributing factor to overeating is the fact that we are not mindful during mealtimes, thus denying ourselves both the oral gratification of taste and texture of our food, as well as neglecting to chew sufficiently or eating rapidly and thereby not allowing the signals of fullness to register within the brain. The act of eating has been diminished and frequent snacking can be an indication of needing oral gratification. How often have you arrived at your destination without being fully aware of how you got there? Have you ever seen someone go sailing through a red traffic light, apparently oblivious to her own actions? Has it never occurred to you that you yourself may have done just that in a moment of distraction, so totally engrossed in your thoughts were you that you were unaware of the world around you? In such instances, not only can a lack of mindfulness be potentially life-threatening, it also robs you of the pleasure of noticing the flowers growing along the route, or the sunbeam radiating through the clouds. And so it is with the journey that we call 'life' — being mindful allows us to observe and experience 'all there is'. Being mindful brings a new meaning to the phrase 'less is more'.

Strangely, having been encouraged to learn the art of doing several things at once in order to keep up with the frenetic pace of modern living, we are also expected to remain focused, the two of which are in total contrast with one another. Whether it is for study purposes, or in order to steadfastly work towards realising our goals, focused attention is essential. It is hardly surprising that so many youngsters are today dependent on mind-altering drugs to enable them to retain a level of attention within the classroom — mindfulness is often discouraged in daily living, and parents display chaotic thought patterns. Very often do we become impatient when a child fails to respond to our call immediately, possibly making a hurtful remark, such as "Are you deaf, or just plain stupid?" Stop for a moment and remember the time long ago when you lost yourself in the magic of what you where doing!

Mental chaos is reflected in the daily routine as well as in the state of material possessions, with many parents complaining that they don't have enough time to become organised, and with homes becoming cluttered and untidy. Children studying in neat and well-organised environments achieve better academic grades, show less violent behaviour, have better sleep patterns, fewer digestive problems and cope better with disturbances. When our minds are disorganised, we live our lives like a hamster on a wheel, frantically trying to catch up with something that doesn't even exist. Our home and family life are accurate reflections of our state of mind!

Take a look around you — is your desk piled high with papers ranging from important to junk mail? Is your fridge-door almost totally covered with little stick-ons, mostly outdated and still not done? Do you forget the really important things in life like remembering a friend's birthday, and have you still not found time to read that fabulous book your Mom sent? Are your bank reconciliations up to date? Do you even know your financial net worth? Is your wardrobe neat and organised, or full of outdated fashions, or two sizes too small? If your mind is chaotic, your life will be too! If you avoid doing tasks because you are unable to find things, or waste money because you don't know what is lurking at the back of your grocery cupboard, you need to de-clutter. Stop looking at your life and ask, "What the heck happened here?" It is *you* who happened, because you don't pay attention to what you are doing in the moment! This doesn't only apply to our material possessions but also to our words and actions! Many of us go through life putting out fires that we started simply because we didn't slow down enough to see the bigger picture, and respond consciously!

Living in the moment helps us to connect the cause and effects in our lives, and to recognise the ramifications of our personal behaviour. We are able to use more of that wonderful innate intelligence, to be guided by our sensitivity, and to really enjoy and savour the fullness of every one of our experiences. Living in the 'now' allows us not only to stop and smell the roses, but to first find the roses amidst the chaos.

Here's a challenge — there are 24 hours in a day, right? You work eight, and use up eight by sleeping and eating; what happens to the other eight? Do you realise that you have between five and eight hours that mysteriously disappear almost every day? When did you last stop to gaze at a rainbow, or watch the clouds moving overhead?

How long is it since you shut out all other distractions and just listened — really listened — to your favourite music? When did you last take a walk and shut out all thoughts — just breathing in air, seeing the scenes, feeling the ground beneath your feet, focusing on or letting go of all tension and allowing the blood to move freely through your veins. Take a piece of fruit, examine its rich colour, texture, smell. Now bite into it — feel the juice, the taste run down you throat, re-examine its texture with your tongue. Be mindful. Eat the fruit. Experience the fruits of life.

How often we hear people say, "Oh, it's just a bad habit!" when referring to their cigarette smoking or overeating! Well, if that's all it is, why not quit the habit? When you are mindful and living in the present moment, you would think before you light up, or before you put that extra biscuit in your mouth. Then breaking bad habits becomes easy!

Being mindful should not be applied only to things of the outer world, but to our inner world of emotions too. So many of my clients, over the years, have come to me suffering from emotional overload, not because their lives have been especially traumatic, but because they have ignored their own feelings. Sadness, grief and anger have cluttered up their very souls and now the process of unpacking it all, dredging up the past, is both necessary and painful. We don't allow time to experience emotions, and we deny our children this opportunity too. We live with a philosophy of 'get over it already!', expecting our children to ignore their physical pain when they fall or their heartache when they are disappointed — yet these are the very core of our human experience! In those fleeting moments before we relinquish our human form, and move through death, that is all we have — our experiences! Not the fancy new dress, not even our acquaintances; only our highs and our lows. The memory of our feelings!

Make a practice of waking up every morning — really waking up and staying awake! Become truly awakened into the new day with all its possibilities and fresh beginnings. Don't allow the poor choices of yesterday, or even yesteryears, to drag you down. Why give more of your precious time to something that is done and can't be undone? Be joyful and grateful that your soul has chosen to spend another day with you, and celebrate. Studying a colony of meercats, you will notice that every morning, shortly before sunrise, these little creatures come out of their burrows and stand upright, facing the east as they greet the new day. And every evening they gather together again, stand facing the west, and acknowledge the passing of another day. Which is the more evolved form of life on Earth?

Begin each day with a song of hope in your heart, and live every moment with a promise — a promise to forgive, to love unconditionally, to make each moment the very best that it can possibly be. Encourage your children to see each day as a new beginning — a chance to succeed where once they failed, a chance to experiment and experience a new way of being, a chance to discover, unveil, the inexhaustible potential which lies within.

It is no use fretting and lamenting the things you wish you had done differently; instead, harness this energy and use it to begin making things right! No matter how bad your relationships may appear, there is nothing, I repeat, nothing, that cannot be fixed with love. For love is a Divine power! If your family relationships are not all that you desire, start the healing process now. Choose words and actions that will mend a broken heart, build bridges of love that will reunite you.

Love, within your own family and relations, love within your heart centre, gives you the power to make real your dreams. Love IS — the source of happiness, peace, health and abundance; it is the power behind creation; it is the innate power within.

Your true self is Divine love. *Namasté*!

Appendix

Holistic Solutions to Common Problems

Each and every case of either physical illness or emotional disharmony is unique in both its cause and treatment, but over the years, I have discovered some common factors which may assist you in dealing with daily health and behavioural issues. The advice given here in no way either precludes nor interferes with Western medicine, but can be used as complimentary healing. By looking beyond the physical, you may be able to treat the cause rather than just the symptom.

Abdominal cramps: Common to younger children, the problem often indicates underlying fear, possibly related to change within the family or routine. If the child is being intimidated at school, or feels unable to cope with the expectations of others, she will frequently manifest as indigestion and tummy ache.

Allergies: Okay, so this is going to upset some folks! Allergies are often a sign that the child is feeling dominated and is unable to express her own power. Where the allergies manifest as hay fever-type symptoms, there is often a perception of being persecuted and judged unfairly. You may have to examine the family dynamics and begin to see each child as a special and unique individual, rather than assuming that all siblings will be similar in character. Nutritionally increase the Vitamin C and Vitamin E intake, and add plenty of fresh carrots (or carrot juice) to the diet.

Appendicitis: Most frequent in pubescent girls, although sometimes also in boys. It demonstrates a fear of the changes precipitated by growth, and confusion regarding the emerging sexuality. Good communication between mother and daughter will help put the subject of sex into proper perspective. Our menstrual cycle is not a curse; it is the first step in the process of creation of life.

Asthma: Often manifests in the over-protected child, where love is literally smothering the child, and stifling her expression. It may also be a sign of sadness and suppressed tears, especially where the child has been ridiculed for crying in the past. Encourage your children to vent their emotions — good or bad — as this will help them to identify their weaknesses and grow from them. Micro-nutrients which may assist are magnesium, Vitamin C, Vitamin B complex and folic acid.

In newborn babies, asthma may indicate that the soul is not yet entirely comfortable in its new role; gentle love will usually help this phase to pass.

Bed wetting: Have the child checked for urinary infection by all means, but in my experience, this usually indicates a fear of a parent, most often of the father! If this rings true, re-assess the level of discipline, and if necessary, seek counselling to rectify the damaged relationship. This may also be a perceived or transferred fear where the child relates to the mother's fear of her husband.

Boils and abscesses: Unresolved anger and resentment are the causes. A single abscess or boil should not cause concern, but when there are repeated incidences, look around for the source. Again this might be due to unfair discipline, but I have also seen it in cases of sexual abuse. Allow your children to speak out — the old belief of 'children should be seen and not heard' is an excuse for emotional abuse! Boils and abscesses are frequently a sign that some bitterness and resentment need to be released.

Chest infections and bronchitis: These are almost always stress related, and the stress invariably stems from an unhappy or volatile family environment. Remind your child a million times a day that she is loved, and accept the love offered to you with reverence! If you, as a parent, suffer from frequent bouts of illnesses, you need to examine your own relationships, particularly with regard to your spouse — there is probably a lack of love in your life.

Colic: Relax more! Your baby senses your impatience and annoyance, even though these are seldom directed at the child. Young mothers who are trying to be 'perfect mothers, perfect wives, perfect housekeepers' often have colic babies — take a look at the relationship between husband and wife, and insist that the husband takes his role as father, protector and provider more seriously. Babies grow very quickly — take time out to really enjoy those few months with your new baby as the laundry can wait, but growth will not! When your children are teenagers, you will wish you had spent more time just cuddling them when they were little! Allowing your baby to spend time without a nappy will encourage kicking and leg-raising movements that help relieve colic. Gently pushing the knees towards the chest often helps too. Consult an aromatherapist about suitable oils for massaging on the stomach area.

Constipation: In small babies, it is often just a sluggish digestive system, or lack of liquid in the diet. Breast-feeding mothers sometimes forget to supplement their child's diet with boiled water or rooibos tea during very hot weather, and toddlers are often not able to discern between hunger and thirst. It may occasionally also indicate a slight Vitamin C deficiency. A quick cure to get the bowels moving is to make the baby lie on her back, nappy off, and gently push the knees towards the chest — this works for all ages, by the way. In older children, frequent constipation may be a sign of not wanting to move forward, but holding on to the past, or wanting things to stay the same, and even trying to recreate circumstances. In all cases increase the intake of water and natural fibres, e.g. fresh fruit, vegetables and cereals. Exercise which massages the abdominal organs is also important as also is walking, running and cycling, or dancing which allows expression at the same time!

Earache and ear infections: Repeated ear infections may lead to deafness and should not be passed over as just a childhood phenomenon! The cause is often simply a case of the child not wanting to hear things — either conflicts in the family, or too many demands being placed on the child.

Eating disorders: Virtually all eating disorders stem from low self-esteem.

Overeating and weight gain: There is a subconscious desire to build a barrier around oneself in order to gain protection, especially from criticism. In teenagers it may be a fear of being rejected by the opposite sex, and of course, as the weight increases, this prophecy is often fulfilled. Both men and women tend to put on weight when they see their lives as being without purpose, and the same applies to children of all ages. It is important for youngsters to have goals —

whether to win a gold at the Olympics, or beat grandfather at chess, or do a cartwheel.

Anorexia and bulimia: These are symptoms of severe self-denial arising from a belief that they are not good enough and therefore undeserving. This may be a result of family problems, but can also be caused when the child is drawn into a 'wrong' circle of friends, does not like what she has become and can't see an escape route. Boost the self-esteem by helping your child to set realistic goals, and assist her in her efforts to achieve them. Both anorexia and bulimia should be regarded as serious — far too many parents ignore them and hope the phase will pass, but without proper counselling it seldom does. Once again, one must look at the parents — if Mom is permanently denying herself in order to stay thin, or making comments at 'sexy slim girls' or derogatory remarks about 'fatties' or siblings being permitted to tease one another about body shape; need I say more? This is particularly important as girls enter puberty, and develop 'puppy fat' — we find it irresistible on puppies, but abhorrent on our own beloved children! A habit of healthy eating within the family will help, as will a gentle discussion about 'not growing upwards so fast any more means you're more inclined to grow outwards'.

Eczema: Are you putting too much pressure on your child to achieve? Allow her to set the pace! Eczema is often an attempt to rid the body of excess stimuli, and is most common in children who try hard to please. This is also an indication of certain dietary deficiencies, especially the essential fatty acids, Vitamin C and zinc. Whilst one might consider what the children could be allergic to in the physical environment, it is well worth questioning what she may be allergic to in her emotional environment!

Eye infections: Quite simple. The child is not happy with what she is seeing! Again take a close look at family relationships, and try not to argue in front of the children. (Yes, children need to learn the realities about long-term relationships, but perhaps your communication levels have been wanting, and the child is not yet able to understand disagreements.) Young children, who are far-sighted, avoid looking at the present, while near-sighted children are fearful of the future. During normal play, the child's eyes will be constantly re-focusing at different distances. For instance, staring at a TV screen strains the eyes by having to hold the lens in a particular state for prolonged periods — just another really good reason to encourage play and limit exposure to TV!

Headaches: Often occurs in the child, or especially in the teenager, who sets very high standards for herself and is full of self-criticism. Make sure to acknowledge achievements, and reassure the child of your unconditional love. Encourage the child to take time out for leisure and rest, and to nurture her own needs. Also often associated with this are sexual fears — guilt or feeling of being pressurised into a sexual relationship. Masturbating can often bring relief. Where stress is a factor, a supplement of magnesium and calcium often works wonders. Sometimes a sluggish digestive tract adds to the problem, so increase the intake of water and fibre. Teenaged girls are notoriously bad eaters, as they begin to watch their weight. Added to this is the fact that the digestive system may not be able to extract calcium from milk beyond the age of around 12 years, so you will need to introduce fermented dairy products like yoghurt and cottage cheese. But this in itself can cause more problems as dairy produce can result in water retention and congestion, so be aware of any common denominators. It is unfortunately a matter of trial and error, but do not rule out the possibility of eye strain! A visit to an optometrist would not be misplaced as the eyes can reveal other underlying problems, such as thyroid imbalance or even pressure on the brain.

Menstrual problems: A rejection of blossoming feminity, perhaps out of fear, guilt or a belief that the genitals and sex are dirty. Your attitude towards your own bodily functions will be a big influence here, and boys and men in the house should be taught to respect the menstrual cycle rather than regard it with disgust. In ancient tradition, a huge celebratory ritual was held in honour of the emergence of womanhood, but today it is shrouded in shame and mystery. Vitamin E has for many years been associated with optimal functioning of the sex organs, and magnesium will certainly assist in relieving menstrual cramps. Once again, exercise which massages the abdominal organs will help — walking, cycling and yoga are especially good.

Miscellaneous aches and pains: A good hug will normally sort this out! It is a cry for love and a longing to be held — children sometimes believe that physical contact is for babies only, and deprive themselves of this very important form of communication.

Nail biting: Frustration, often caused by domineering parents or circumstances that appear to be beyond control. Life is not a race, and we should all have time in our daily routine to 'stand still' while we lie and watch the clouds go by, listen to music or meditate. Encourage your children to do this, and ensure that their activities are not excessive. It may even be done to spite the parents as seen in younger children; older children usually take more drastic measures, like bulimia!

Nose bleeds: This can be crying out for love. Again hug your child! Vitamin C deficiency and anaemia may be interfering with the normal clotting process, especially in young girls who have started to menstruate.

Overeating in small children: Seen particularly at parties where there may be an abundance of goodies not normally available to the child. The child may have a fear of not having her primary needs met, or may feel insecure and judgemental towards herself. Parents frequently make the mistake of using food as a pacifier — reward good behaviour with a treat, or give the child a sweet to help her overcome a disappointment, or 'fix' a scraped knee, etc. In the long run, this will most likely lead to eating problems later in life, and the child should rather be comforted or congratulated by teaching her self-gratification or 'feel good' techniques. Reassure your child that she is special and unique and that you love her just the way she is! Perhaps, you have been too strict about not allowing treats in the house, and might need to loosen up a little in this regard. All through life the tendency to overeat during times of stress is an attempt to block the real emotions — a way of self-gratification that actually delays the process of acknowledgment and victory over these emotions.

If the child appears to be constantly hungry, a good tonic will go a long way towards alleviating any deficiencies, such as those of zinc or iron, and in fact I recommend that all children take a daily vitamin/mineral supplement.

Skin conditions (***acne and blackheads***): Usually striking during puberty, it reveals a tendency to be unsure of oneself, even disliking oneself, often accompanied by a belief that she is 'dirty'. As the hormones kick in, body odour changes. Boys frequently have wet dreams, and girls begin to have vaginal discharge. Hopefully you have instilled good personal hygiene, but your teenager may shower three times a day in an attempt to 'stay clean' or not at all as a way of 'denying' that these changes are real! Lead by example! Diet obviously plays an important role here — essential fatty acids, Vitamin B complex (good ol' Brewers' yeast) and zinc are often deficient. Plenty of Vitamin C will improve the elasticity of the skin, ensuring that the pores are able to open and close freely, and fresh carrots (or better still, fresh carrot juice) will provide an ample source of Vitamin A, as well as antioxidants. Many teenagers become frustrated because they do all the right things — eat lots of fruit and vegetables, take regular exercise and cleanse properly, yet the problem remains. Unfortunately hormones play havoc with our skin and that's the truth. However, boys often benefit from taking a zinc supplement — large quantities are lost through perspiration in the active teenager, and enormous amounts are required for the healthy development of the genitals and production of sperm. Dandruff is often a confirmation of low zinc levels. Later on in life, poor zinc status can result in low libido, especially in sportsmen.

Sleep: There are five essential elements for a good and healthy life — food, water, air, attitude and rest. Our bodies do all sorts of maintenance work while we sleep — repairing and growing being just two of them. Some families have a belief that sleeping is laziness, hence they never allow a child to lie in or take an afternoon nap. I say 'let them sleep', and research has shown that teenagers require almost as much sleep as babies! Nevertheless, sleep can be a form of escapism and you need to be on the lookout for other signs of depression or anti-social behaviour. A child who is 'always tired' should be checked for anaemia. In smaller children, sudden changes in the sleep pattern can be an indication of serious health problems and should be brought to the attention of your paediatrician or family doctor.

Stuttering: Here we go again with my campaign to get unpopular with parents! Allow your child plenty of space for self-expression, and reserve your comments! Listen to your child — what she has to say IS important, always! Also, very important, allow your child to cry — boy or girl — as this is the ultimate in self-expression! Never threaten or punish a child for stuttering, and resist the temptation to 'speak for them', thus negating the importance of what they have to say. As wacky as this might sound to some, I once had a client who suffered as a result of *karmic* issues brought forward from a previous life — a deep subconscious fear of speaking for fear of being punished! If all else fails, consider regression or hypnotherapy.

Throat infections: Inability to speak up for oneself, or alternatively a tendency to gossip and tell untruths! Where this problem escalates to tonsilitis, the child is repressing emotions — often occurs when the child feels she is being overlooked in favour of siblings. Increasingly a problem with children from broken homes who would like to say, "What about me?" but don't know how! Also appears to be more frequent in the oldest child who might feel that she is not getting the individual attention she got before the arrival of a younger brother or sister. Remember, small children are often wiser than their vocabulary allows them to display, and so other forms of expression, such as drawing and play, are vital.

Unexplained fevers: Never ignore a fever in a young child and try to look for underlying causes of anger which include leaving the child alone, making her feel unfairly treated, or even, rejected.